REVERSING
DISCRIMINATION

REVERSING DISCRIMINATION

The Case for

Affirmative Action

GERALD HORNE

INTERNATIONAL PUBLISHERS, New York

FOR the U.S. LEFT

The cartoons herein are reprinted with
permission from Brumsic Brandon, Jr.
and Freedomways *magazine.*

Library of Congress Cataloging-in-Publication Data

Horne, Gerald.
    Reversing discrimination : the case for affirmative action /
Gerald Horne.
        p.   cm.
    Includes bibliographical references.
    ISBN 0-7178-0695-2 : $6.95
    1. Affirmative action programs--Law an legislation--United States
I. Title.
KF3464.H67   1992
342.73'0873--dc20
[347.302873]   92-20622

Contents

*Illustrations on pages ii, vi,
viii, 16, 36, 58, 86, 112, 116*

"NONRACIAL"

REVERSING DISCRIMINATION

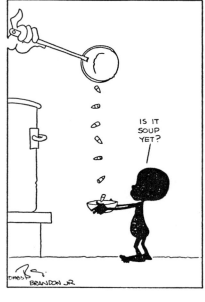

Introduction

Affirmative action is the name given to a number of policies designed to overcome past and present discrimination and provide opportunity for those traditionally denied it. Although African Americans are often singled out as the sole beneficiary of affirmative action, the fact is that recipients have included Latinos, Asian-Americans, Pacific Islanders, Native Americans and—perhaps the most significant beneficiary—non-ethnic minority women. It is apparent that the effort to point to affirmative action as a "black program" and not what it is, i.e., a program designed to benefit the nation's majority, is just another effort to build on racial resentments backed by centuries of "Afro-phobia" in order to hamper steps toward equality.

Affirmative action in this country traditionally has been limited to employment and education. Yet, in the broadest sense affirmative action can be viewed as any conscious efforts to reverse discrimination. Most often in the U.S., however, affirmative action is the term used to describe such relatively benign steps as insuring that job openings are advertised in mass media usually read by affirmative action recipients, e.g., *MS.* magazine or the *Washington Afro-American;* or fire departments setting up tables in Harlem to insure that job openings are brought to the attention of African Americans; or a university making special steps to insure that schools in heavily Latino East Los Angeles receive their brochures. Affirmative action can also mean that employers or schools must meet goals and timetables to make sure that their labor force or student body is racially and ethnically diverse and gender balanced. As we approach the 21st century and it becomes clear that a larger percentage of the work force will be oppressed minorities and non-minority women, affirmative action looms as not a matter of charity but a tool to insure economic viability. Otherwise this

1

nation runs the risk of apartheid-style economic gridlock, where the bulk of the country does not have the skill to propel a complex economy nor the capital to consume what is produced. Affirmative action in employment means not only mechanisms to move ethnic minorities and non-minority women into positions from which they have been traditionally excluded. It also entails upgrading those jobs to which they are routinely consigned. Similarly, affirmative action does not mean only insuring that the previously excluded are admitted to Ivy League schools; it also means that, for example, historically Black institutions are upgraded dramatically.

Affirmative action can be seen as the remedy for discrimination. When there is bias, there must be a remedy. Discrimination is the enemy of democracy; hence, affirmative action is a core component of the ongoing struggle for democracy. And the path to socialism is paved with the struggle for democracy; but affirmative action would not cease with the proclamation of socialism; if anything, it would accelerate.

Quotas

Though often denounced in ritual fashion, affirmative action has actually been part of our society for decades. For example, in cities like New York there has traditionally been an effort by political parties to put forward a so-called "balanced ticket" that included, an Irish-American, Italian-American, Jewish-American, et.al. This was seen as part and parcel of democratic practice. There was no clamor about this being a so-called "quota" system or maunderings about how such a process negated "merit." Curiously enough, it was only when African Americans began to demand inclusion on such "balanced tickets" that this kind of demagogy arose.

Similarly, affirmative action often is denounced as "reverse discrimination" against Euro-American males. This is curious thinking. When buildings are forced to build ramps for the physically challenged or lifts for buses are mandated, is this "reverse discrimination?" Does the cinema engage in "reverse discrimination" when it charges children and senior citizens less to be admitted? Is it "reverse discrimination" when veterans receive special benefits from the government? Curiously, the concept of "reverse discrimination" seems to arise only when programs that are perceived as benefiting African Americans are considered.

Affirmative action is necessary because of the past and present discrimination perpetrated primarily by a monopoly capitalist class that has sought to *profit* from the fruits of bigotry and to benefit politically from keeping the working class divided. Though there are working-class whites who oppose affirmative action and some capitalists who support it, this should not obscure the basic fact that affirmative action would be secure today but for fierce opposition overwhelmingly from the right wing of the capitalist class.

Demagogues also have sought to cloud the question of use of goals by suggesting that this actually means the use of rigid "quotas," which allegedly would mean selection of "unqualified" minorities or non-minority women above "qualified" Euro-American males. Indeed, this charge has come to be a staple of electoral campaigns in this country and has been used most adroitly by the Republican Party. However, this charge is fallacious in many senses. Though the allegation about selection of the "unqualified" is often tossed about, evidence to substantiate this incendiary charge is lacking precisely because—as shall be outlined below—determining who is or is not "qualified" is difficult to do with mathematical precision in most instances. For example, some would argue that a man with a college degree is more qualified to be a truck driver that a woman with a high school degree but there is no inherent reason why this should be so. Is it fair to say that a student with an A⁻ average from Beverly Hills is more qualified to be admitted to college than a student with a B average from East Los Angeles, who had to overcome numerous hurdles? Most of all, this debate about qualifications obscures the real fact that institutionalized racism and sexism serve as a barrier to exclude non-minority women, racial and ethnic minorities—which is why affirmative action is necessary in the first place. In any event, quotas should not be ruled out as a remedy to address particularly noxious forms of discrimination.

Righting Wrong

Though affirmative action in this country is limited generally to employment and education, there is no reason why it should not be extended into other arenas. In India, for example, the "harijans" or so-called lowest castes have set-asides not only in the university but also in Parliament. In the U.S., as a remedy for housing discrimination, courts have sought to force municipalities in New Jersey to build housing for the low income families who are disproportionately ethnic minority in that state. This can be seen as a form of affirmative action. One challenge for the future is extending affirmative action across the board, since discrimination is not limited to just employment and education. Indeed, if the scope of affirmative action is not extended widely, then the areas where it is *not* extended— e.g., health care, housing, etc.—will wind up negating process in those areas where it is in place.

One of the earliest forms of affirmative action could be considered the heralded "40 acres and a mule" that should have been allocated to former slaves upon their emancipation. Like affirmative action, such a program would have served as an antidote to racism while seeking to bring the formerly excluded into the economic mainstream. Moreover, this program was targeted at former slaves and thus could not be considered "reverse discrimination" against those who were not beneficiaries.

Recalling this 19th century initiative also reminds us that affirmative action is manifestly a product of struggle, and has not been handed to its recipients on a silver platter. The 14th Amendment to the U.S. Constitution—which is the main juridical basis for affirmative action insofar as it mandates "equal protection under the law"—was a product of struggle and intense wrangling when passed after the Civil War.[1] And just as "40 acres and a mule" wound up being an unkept promise as the political correlation of forces changed, today's affirmative action, too, can be overthrown without eternal vigilance. Struggle—or more specifically a threat of a march on Washington —forced President Franklin Roosevelt to issue an Executive Order that sought to bar discriminatory practices among government contractors. Struggle, or more specifically the march on Washington of 1963, also led to passage of the Civil Rights Act of 1964, yet another legal basis for affirmative action. Struggle, or more specifically the massive marches and demonstrations of the 1960s, caused President Lyndon Johnson to issue another Executive Order that also serves as a legal basis for affirmative action. Struggle, or more specifically the Selma to Montgomery March, led directly to the passage of the Voting

Rights Act of 1965, which has brought a form of affirmative action to the reapportionment of state legislatures/Congress, and other electoral bodies seeking to insure that ethnic minority districts are created or not diluted.

Rise in Racism

Affirmative action is designed to serve as an antidote to discrimination. Though some would argue that patterns of institutionalized bigotry are a thing of the past, in fact the opposite is the case; thus, this book will—inter alia—seek to document the ingrained patterns of discrimination that make the struggle for affirmative action more pressing than ever. Indeed, the advent of the Reagan-Bush Administrations has led to a veritable explosion of discrimination. When Ronald Reagan opened his 1980 campaign for President in Philadelphia, Mississippi—the town where Klansmen and police murdered civil rights workers in 1964—a signal was sent that the time had come to reverse the gains of the civil rights movement. When his administration broke the Professional Air Traffic Controllers strike early in his tenure, another signal was sent that all of the gains of working people—including the right to organize trade unions— were in jeopardy.

Thus, the past decade has seen a proliferation of racist violence and misogyny. This trend reached a crescendo in November 1991 when David Duke, he of the Nazi and Ku Klux Klan background, received 55% of the white vote in the gubernatorial race in Louisiana. In New York City racist mobs have lynched African American youth who happened to wander into the "wrong" neighborhood. In her best-selling book, *Backlash*, Susan Faludi details how sexism was stoked repeatedly, particularly by powerful forces within the mass media. At the same time, a massive redistribution of wealth from bottom to top took place, and to distract attention from this act of class warfare the energy of all too many was diverted into racist and sexist binges. This atmosphere facilitated an erosion of affirmative action and a worsening of the standard of living of oppressed minorities—and the entire working class—while the "feminization of poverty" became more than a slogan to many women.

International developments also facilitated this trend. *The epochal political changes in Eastern Europe have devalued the use of anti-communism as a divisive weapon and increased the value of racism.* The increase in inter-imperialist contradictions has focused on Japan and "Japan bashing," which has given the "race card" new meaning. In a recent report of the U.S. Civil Rights Commission entitled *Civil Rights Issues Facing Asian-Americans in the 1990s,* it was noted that the Japan-bashing engaged in by Lee Iacocca and other fat cats has fed not only bias against Japanese-Americans but against minorities generally.

Affirmative action has been one of the more useful weapons wielded against both "white supremacy" and "male supremacy," or the long-standing notion in this country that there has been a veritable "divine right" of certain Euro-American men to rule, to have the best jobs, and the highest standard of living.

This trend must be resisted by the working class, above all, for bigotry benefits the boss while affirmative action unifies the working class. When a sector of the working class can be stigmatized on the basis of race, ethnicity or gender and forced to work for less, *this drags down the wage level for the entire class.* At times this is easier to see on the international level. When workers in Bangladesh and Georgia are making textiles, in a sense they are made to compete against each other, and the paltry wages paid the former inevitably drags down the wage level and working conditions of the latter. Ineluctably textile manufacturers would gravitate toward Bangladesh because of cheaper costs; hence, the growing phenomenon of "runaway shops." Therefore, it is in the best interests of those Georgia workers to support a militant labor movement in Bangladesh and elsewhere so that labor standards in South Asia and everywhere can rise—i.e., labor solidarity can be seen as another form of affirmative action. This also suggests that the ultimate safeguard for affirmative action at home is equity abroad. Thus, those policies of the AFL-CIO that have leaned toward supporting anti-communist regimes and opposing progressive labor movements have been harmful to the U.S. working class. This is why *"workers of the world unite"* remains a viable slogan, despite the alleged "collapse of communism" and why affirmative action to raise wages and working conditions globally should be an absolute priority for the U.S. working class.

This principle can also be applied domestically. Once it was stated: "Labor cannot emancipate itself in the white skin where in the black skin it is branded."[2] Uplifting those in the U.S.

working class who have suffered discrimination is of ultimate benefit to the entire class. There are those who feel that such invidious discrimination actually benefits that sector of the working class that is comprised of Euro-American males; however, though they may receive some sort of short-term psychic benefit, like a rush of crack cocaine it eventually wears off and leaves the user in a worse condition. If discrimination were of benefit to this sector of white male workers, one would expect those in Mississippi to be better off than their counterparts in Detroit; but this is not the case. One reason is that discrimination also hinders the formation of trade unions, which have been one of the more reliable vehicles for raising wages; and the South traditionally—not least because of bigotry—has been the bastion of anti-union "right to work" (for less) laws.

Consequently, affirmative action is in the long-term interest of the working class. Some argue that this is a form of "reverse discrimination" against white male workers; one writer, Frederick Lynch, has penned a book, *Invisible Victims*, that purports to describe their plight. However, one reason these "victims" may be "invisible" is that they may not exist. For example, when Denny Green, an African American, was named head coach of the Minnesota Vikings football team, a white male conceivably could argue that affirmative action had deprived him of that post. However, when Dave Shula, a relatively inexperienced and youthful white male, was named head coach of the Cincinnatti Bengals, such a charge would not ensue. The implicit premise is that white males are always deserving but others never are and, in fact, should remain at the bottom of the socioeconomic ladder. In other words, it is fine if a fellow white male gets the post but a horror if anyone else does. In any case, it has been suggested by Gertrude Ezorsky in her worthwhile *Racism & Justice: The Case for Affirmative Action* that if a white male can actually prove that some allegedly "unqualified" oppressed minority or non-minority woman received a post over a white male, then the latter should be allowed to dip into a specially constructed government fund for compensation. However, it is doubtful if such a case could be made.

Democracy

If anything, affirmative action should be seen as yet another mechanism that democratizes the entire system and thereby brings gains to the entire class. For example, African Americans principally pushed for the Civil Rights Act of 1964 and its progeny; yet, the beneficiaries have gone far beyond this sector to include non-minority women, other oppressed minorities, et. al.

Perhaps the most significant beneficiary of anti-discrimination laws have been white males over the age of 55 who have invoked laws against age discrimination when rapacious employers have sought to replace them with youth who make far less. It has been suggested that judges, who disproportionately come from this group, have a special sympathy for such plaintiffs.

Likewise, when the civil rights movement—which was disproportionately, though not exclusively, comprised of African Americans—pushed for laws that sought to overturn requirements for jobs that were not work-related, the entire working class benefited. For example, why should a firefighter know Shakespeare—so he/she could chant sonnets and thereby soothe one who is being rescued? Obviously, this requirement was not job related and tended to invidiously impact not only African Americans but all who had been deprived of such levels of education. Affirmative action has led to a situation where jobs, at least theoretically, should be advertised widely, hence increasing the pool of applicants and curbing the "old boy network" that has excluded not only racial and ethnic minorities and non-minority women but white males who were not properly "connected." For example, at one time to receive a post in the Sociology Department at the University of California–Santa Barbara, a senior professor at the University of Chicago would call a colleague at that campus to recommend one of his students. Such an inbred process excluded many, not just African Americans. With affirmative action, this process has been opened up to all and not limited just to a narrow circle.

In sum, affirmative action has meant the broadening of the pool of applicants for jobs. This also undermines the canard that affirmative action has led to illegal quotas. In any case, the quotas of the past that, for example, tended to exclude many Jewish-Americans were ceilings or a *maximum* that set a limit on their rise. Affirmative action goals, in contrast, set a floor or a *minimum* number that employers are welcome to exceed. Moreover, affirmative action insures only that the pool of applicants should be diversified, it does not necessarily insure which person should be hired—and this can be seen as a weakness of affirmative action. This also illustrates the emptiness of the claims of affirmative action opponents who consistently turn reality on its head.

Similarly, when African American students at Rutgers University started pressing for admission of more from their community in the 1960s, the state of New Jersey responded by expanding the system of higher education. Livingston College was created, along with Ramapo College and a number of other campuses. This meant jobs for construction workers, professors, administrators, cafeteria workers, janitors, and a host of others. Only a small percentage of these beneficiaries were African American. This is why the African-American-led civil rights movement has been characterized as one of the most altruistic movements of all time, in that it opened so many doors for non-Blacks. And this makes even more ironic the cry of "reverse discrimination" from certain circles.

Collective Remedies

Affirmative action is not only an antidote for discrimination and a means to include the previously excluded in the mainstream, it is also a form of compensation for disfiguring bigotry. In the same light, Japanese Americans who were subjected to an unconstitutional incarceration during World War II were provided with what can only be termed an attempt at compensation, $20,000 each; this amount was not provided to other U.S. citizens because they were not subjected to this kind of heinous violation. Was this "reverse discrimination" against those non-Japanese Americans who did not receive such a payout? Similarly, African Americans were subjected to slavery, racial discrimination, Jim Crow and the like, which inevitably has hampered progress for an entire people. Affirmative action is an attempt at compensation for this injury. In that sense, affirmative action is in the broad tradition of U.S. law that seeks to provide remedies for wrongs. If slavery and Jim Crow were "wrong," (which few besides Pat Buchanan and David Duke would deny) then U.S. law demands that there must be a remedy. Affirmative action is that remedy.

Affirmative action is a group remedy for a group wrong. When a Mexican American is denied a job because of national origin discrimination, this wrong is committed not because the perpetrator had a particular animus against that particular person; indeed, the perpetrator most likely hardly knows the individual in question. The discrimination is visited upon the individual because he/she is a member of a group. The essence of bigotry is this kind of collective punishment. It is the same principle that leads the Israeli Defense Force to bulldoze Palestinian homes randomly when any Palestinian commits a presumed offense.

Yet, the right-wing has argued against affirmative action precisely because it is a collective remedy. Clarence Thomas, recently appointed to the U.S. Supreme Court, has argued that such collective remedies deny his individuality. However, once again Justice Thomas reveals only how little he actually knows about the law, for racism operates beyond the individual level, which is why a group remedy like affirmative action is so necessary.

This point was dramatized in one of the more key affirmative action cases that reached the U.S. Supreme Court, *United Steelworkers of America v. Weber* (1979). Kernell Goudia, an African American worker, in an affidavit commented on how racial discrimination led to his lacking the "prior experience" requirement set by Kaiser Aluminum for skilled jobs:

> In 1968, upon discharge from the armed services, I applied to LSU trade school. I was sent an invitation to come for an interview, but when I appeared and was seen in person, I was told I would not be interviewed. Louisiana had a system of segregated trade schools, and out of the 27 schools in the state, only two accepted Blacks and their programs were limited to traditionally Black jobs. I had always been interested in getting craft training but due to discrimination was barred. I understood Kaiser had required prior experience to get into craft positions or training positions, but given the situation in Louisiana this requirement all but excluded Blacks.[3]

Hence, African Americans in the South and elsewhere have faced a cruel dilemma: they have been barred from receiving training for certain posts because of bigotry and then are

barred from receiving certain jobs because they have not received the requisite training! When special programs are initiated in the form of affirmative action to overcome this obstacle,
they are pilloried as forms of "reverse discrimination."

Housing discrimination often is pointed to as one of the more
pernicious forms of discrimination; its continued existence is
one reason why affirmative action in both employment and education remain so necessary. Housing discrimination is one of
the main factors contributing to Latinos and African Americans
particularly receiving segregated and inadequate education
that often bars them from admission to college and higher level
jobs. When busing was promoted as a remedy to overcome the
barrier of housing discrimination leading to inadequate education, this remedy was widely denounced in racist campaigns.
Housing discrimination leads to the creation of "ghettos" where
fewer tax dollars are spent on, e.g., libraries. Increasingly many
jobs are being placed in suburbs far from the areas where many
African-Americans and Latinos reside; most cities do not have
mass transit systems on a scale that can overcome this barrier.

It should be clear that housing discrimination is no accident
of history but the result of racist policies. This has been elabo-
rated on significantly by Kenneth Jackson in his *Crabgrass
Frontier*, where he details how government policies facilitated
and promoted racial discrimination. Real estate agencies have
engaged in "racial steering" i.e., steering racial and ethnic minorities toward certain neighborhoods and away from others.
Banks have engaged in redlining or allowing many African
American and Latino neighborhoods to wither on the vine by
not providing loan capital for mortgages and home improve-
ment.

One can detail an entire pattern of racist and sexist discrimination in areas as diverse as education, housing, health, access
to capital, etc. Affirmative action is one small step to override
this horrible pattern. Such patterns also help to place the question of merit in proper perspective. For if some have suffered
discrimination, this fact suggests that others have received an
unfair advantage. For example, the African National Congress
is quick to point out that the Boers in South Africa constructed
one of the most successful affirmative action programs in history to bolster their white brethren. Consider the baseball play-

ers who before 1946 were able to get to the Hall of Fame more easily since they did not have to compete against the Bob Gibsons and Juan Marichals of their era. Moreover, past patterns of discrimination means that even with affirmative action many non-minority families enjoy advantages in wealth that not only can be passed on to their children but can be parlayed into educational and vocational advantages for the entire family. Either affirmative action is pursued or we run the risk of freezing in place a devastating institutionalized bigotry.

The Myth of Meritocracy

It is suggested at times that affirmative action subverts the notion of a meritocracy. This is a curious claim. It is well known that under monopoly capitalism there is a tendency for connections to replace competition. It is well known that "who you know" is often more important than "what you know" in obtaining a position. The notion of a meritocracy is just another myth. Are judges in New York City selected on the basis of merit or selected because of their connections to various political clubhouses? When the "same old white guys" are recycled for various coaching positions in college and professional sports, is this a question of merit or just another example of discrimination writ large? When the friends and relatives of the well-connected are selected for apprenticeship posts that lead to membership in craft unions, while non-minority women and racial minorities are barred, is this a question of merit or just another example of discrimination? When women are barred from coal mining jobs because they are women and not because of merit, is this not discrimination?

In any case, past and present discrimination are the reasons why the recipients of affirmative action often lack certain requirements—e.g., diplomas, certificates, test scores, and the like—to qualify for certain jobs. Jonathan Kozol in *Savage Inequalities* writes movingly about how schools attended by African Americans in East St. Louis, Illinois have significantly less funding and facilities than schools in the predominantly white suburbs of Chicago. Affirmative action, then, becomes a tool to level the playing field and overcome that formidable barrier of discrimination.

The question of merit is deployed insidiously in the context of admissions to universities. In this society, college education has become increasingly widespread and is a requirement for many skilled jobs; production workers often upgrade their skills at junior colleges. Affirmative action programs are in place at many schools to try to insure that there is a diverse student body. These programs can involve the discounting of scores on standardized tests. This is necessary because there are a number of companies, e.g. Stanley Kaplan, Inc., that for a pretty penny will instruct those who can afford to pay on how to do well on these tests; this means that many of these tests do not measure the scope of the intellect as much as they measure the depth of the pocketbook. Needless to say, many of those who cannot afford Kaplan are oppressed minorities. And just as these minorities often have had to suffer through inadequate schools that ill prepare them for standardized tests, recent studies show that girls of whatever nationality receive second-class treatment in the classroom, which hampers their educational performance.

Then there is the question of the substance of these tests. A number of studies have pointed to the existence of cultural bias in these tests. For example, many of these tests involve the use of word analogies, e.g., "cup is to saucer is as (a) bat is to ball or (b) lamp is to table." Many homes in this nation have neither cups nor saucers, many girls are not as familiar with bats and balls as boys are. Educational psychologists suggest that because one cannot answer such questions to the satisfaction of the test-maker does not necessarily indicate an inferior intellect on the part of the test taker. Yet, such tests are used on a daily basis as a filter to screen out otherwise competent and qualified applicants.

It is also curious that when test scores and grades are discounted for sons and daughters of alumni of certain colleges, no hue and cry is raised; this group is disproportionately comprised of white people, who, after all, have been the main group attending college and are in a position today to be deemed alumni. This substantiates the idea that opposition to affirmative action often is fueled by notions of "white supremacy" or the idea that those of European descent have a "divine right" to enjoy the fruits of this society and all others should aspire to be no more than hewers of wood or drawers of water. Furthermore, it is well known that big donors to colleges often have an advantage in placing their offspring in said colleges, irrespective of test scores and grades. Yet this has not been the subject of massive outcry.

Further, certain East Coast institutions seek geographic diversity, particularly as population has shifted west. Thus, a student from Montana may have a better chance of being admitted in one of these schools than a student from New Jersey, even if the latter has better test scores or grades. But no one has raised the question of "reverse discrimination" against New Jerseyites. Thus, colleges seek diversity, and not just of the racial, ethnic and gender variety. If they have teachers instructing in areas like electrical engineering or Spanish or Yiddish, they must seek out students with those interests, and such students may be admitted with lower tests scores or grades over a student whose interests are overrepresented in the student, body, e.g., one who seeks to major in business. Once again, it is curious that on college campuses only measures to push racial diversity tend to cause controversy while measures to insure other forms of diversity go unremarked.

Double Standards

A similar curiosity is engendered when one considers other programs that can be analogized to affirmative action but do not stoke as much outrage. Consider veterans' preference, for example; it operates to give veterans of the U.S. armed forces preference for a host of government programs, e.g. government backed mortgages for home ownership. It is buttressed by a range of other programs such as hospitals and educational benefits for veterans. Why is this not considered "reverse discrimination" against non-veterans not eligible for such benefits? Furthermore, these programs tend to favor men over women. Obviously, the determination has been made that veterans have had to bear a special burden and thus deserve a special compensation as a result—akin to oppressed minorities and non-minority women.

Affirmative action is a government initiative that has sought to bring benefit to those traditionally barred from any form of government largesse. Agri-business receives massive subsidies from the government; dollars that could have gone to education and health. Textile manufacturers benefit from tariffs on imports placed by the government. Lee Iacocca and other auto industry fat cats have demanded all manner of restrictions on Japanese exports to this country, including goals, timetables, quotas and the like. Those who argue that affirmative action overrides merit have not made a similar argument about overriding the merit of Japanese exports.

There are other distortions often made of affirmative action. It has already been shown that it is not a program just for African Americans, as is so often suggested. There is another wrinkle in this discourse that suggests that only "middle class" Blacks benefit from affirmative action. Given the lack of precision with which the term "middle class" is used, it is often unclear what is meant. Still, the fact remains that in the area of employment, affirmative action has had some of its most significant impact in government hiring—police and fire departments. It is no accident that one of the most significant affirmative action cases to reach the U.S. Supreme Court involved the United Steelworkers of America. Above all, in a political and philosophical sense, affirmative action has been of the most benefit to the working class as a whole.

It is also suggested that affirmative action reinforces prejudice and helps to inject a note of self-doubt among recipients concerning their self-worth and merit. This was a major theme of the insipid book by Shelby Steele, *The Content of our Character* and the similarly weak *Reflections of an Affirmative Action Baby* by Steven Carter. Curiously, both books—which are written by African Americans—assume that only African Americans experience self-doubt. Necessarily, the "evidence" for such propositions is heavily anecdotal. One wonders why these writers do not pen tomes about how Lee Iacocca experiences self-doubt because his company requires government aid. It is not affirmative action that causes the prejudice but, ultimately, it is monopoly capitalism that breeds it. Again, such books are just another scurrilous attempt to throw dust in the eyes of the public.

To conclude, affirmative action must be seen as part of the ongoing struggle for democracy and, as such, paves the way for socialism. Racism, sexism and other forms of bigotry are the enemy of democracy and their continued existence underscores why affirmative action is one of the key struggles of this era.

1.

The General Landscape for Affirmative Action

The government—executive, legislature and judicial—has been critical in propelling or blocking the trajectory of affirmative action. Recall that the 14th Amendment, passed after the Civil War, has served as the legal basis for affirmative action. Recall that Executive Orders penned by FDR and LBJ have played a similar role. Recall the Civil Rights Act of 1964 passed by the House and the Senate, and Supreme Court decisions in such key cases as *Weber* and *Bakke*.

Keeping this framework in mind, one must be quite concerned about the future trajectory of affirmative action. Take the U.S. Supreme Court, for example. The addition of the reactionary Clarence Thomas as a replacement for Thurgood Marshall has strengthened the ultra-right bloc that has dominated the high court. But even before Thomas's untimely arrival there was cause for concern. The *Los Angeles Times* of 29 September 1991 noted that Chief Justice William Rehnquist has carried a peculiar animus toward affirmative action:

> On matters involving the Constitution, Rehnquist's hands-off approach has been extraordinarily consistent. There is, however, one major exception: affirmative action. Repeatedly, and without exception, he has voted to strike down laws—city, state or federal—that give preferences to blacks, women, Latinos or other minorities. Whether it is the University of California giving an edge in admissions to minority students, the Federal Communications Commission giving a slight preference to minorities in competing for broadcast licenses.... Rehnquist says those laws are unconstitutional. White males are entitled to "the equal protection of the laws," too, he says.

The problem with Rehnquist's analysis is that it is inconsistent.

Forty years ago he did not think discrimination against African-American school children was unconstitutional. Twenty years ago he argued that discrimination against women was not unconstitutional. Yet today he insists stridently that affirmative action violates the Constitution. This is even more bizarre since the Chief Justice rarely strikes down any law on the ground that it violates the Constitution.

According to the Chief Justice, the state may execute juveniles for murder, may arrest gays for homosexual acts in their homes and may prevent women from having abortions; however, the state cannot allow affirmative action. During the 1988-89 term when the court was split on all manner of cases involving flag burning, the death penalty, drug testing, abortion, religion, etc., Rehnquist voted against the government only once: to prevent the city of Richmond, Virginia from applying an ordinance that provided affirmative action for minority business.

This is not just a matter of passing concern. For if unions or even businesses seek to include an affirmative action clauses in labor contracts—as some have sought to do—the danger remains that it can be thrown out as illegal. This danger is magnified when one considers that the Reagan-Bush Administrations have sought to appoint federal judges in the image of the Chief Justice. Among the 126 judicial appointees of George Bush, 3/4 had a net worth of more than $500,000; by contrast, "only" 45% of Reagan's appointees were so well off and 17% of Jimmy Carter's appointees. According to the Alliance for Justice, Bush has made only a "lackluster" effort to choose non-minority women and racial or ethnic minorities for judgeships. In any case, Bush and Reagan have appointed 440 of the 837 lifetime federal judgeships; their appointees form the majority on the Supreme Court and on all but 2 of the 13 federal Circuit Courts.[1]

Because of this utter domination of the federal courts by right wing clones, the idea has mushroomed among unions that cases should be kept out of these courts whenever possible, and state courts and the legislature should be utilized. Generally, this is a sound tactic but even here problems arise. For example, a judicial commission in New York that spent three years and $1 million studying the question concluded that the New

York state court system is "infested with racism." They noted that minorities are less likely to serve on juries and less likely to receive favorable action from the courts; minority attorneys encounter bias and stereotypes in court. Moreover, the courts themselves are in dire need of affirmative action in that minorities share only 4% of the technical jobs, including judgeships. Simultaneously, 22% of the state's population are oppressed minorities, while the prison population is 82% minority.[2]

Though many of these judges prate endlessly about merit, it is well known that selection for these judgeships have nothing to do with that hallowed principle. One example should suffice. New York Supreme court Justice Robert L. Nahman is in that lofty post primarily because of a political relationship with Queens County Democratic chairman Thomas Manton.[3]

If this were not bad enough, a recent survey by the NAACP Legal Defense and Educational Fund and the National Employment Lawyers Association found that minorities in particular are having a harder time finding lawyers willing to take their job discrimination cases. This is in the wake of a spate of Supreme Court decisions that made it more difficult to bring such cases. According to Attorney Fred Gittes, "Fewer and fewer lawyers are doing civil rights work, which makes it impossible for those suffering from discrimination to do anything about it."[4] Hence, if a Latino worker is fired illegally from her job or if a union is forced to defend an affirmative action plan in court, they may find that there is no lawyer to take the case and even if there is, they may have to come before a right-wing judge in a racist court.

The tone for this turn to the right has been set by the Republican Party and George Bush. In a highly publicized speech, Senator Bill Bradley of New Jersey charged that Bush "hasn't been above using race to get votes in a divisive way at a number of points in his career." He recalled Bush's opposition to the 1964 Civil Rights Act, a bedrock foundation for affirmative action.[5] The "success" of Reagan and Bush have encouraged other politicians to travel down the same "quota"-bashing road. David Duke and Patrick Buchanan come quickly to mind but they are just the most highly publicized examples. Consider "white separatist" and former Nazi leader Ralph Forbes who was campaign manager for Duke's 1988 presidential race and who won 46% of the vote in 1990 in the Arkansas GOP primary for lieutenant governor. Consider Kirk Fordice who was elected Governor of Mississippi in 1991. A prime issue of his was opposition to affirmative action; he was the "driving force behind a 10-year challenge to an Army Corps of Engineers program to set aside some contracts" for minority businesses. He also was a driving force in *Richmond v. Croson,* which has been the most harmful decision for affirmative action to this point.[6] The success of these right-wing clones has even encouraged some African American solons to jump on this bandwagon. The moving force to gut welfare in the New Jersey state legislature has been the 43-year-old Black legislator, Wayne Bryant. This opportunist virus is spreading. As reported in the 11 April 1992 *Peoples Weekly World,* erstwhile Senator John Kerry of Massachusetts has been speaking out vigorously against affirmative action, implying that it is a program aimed solely for African Americans.

Congress, under mass pressure from unions and civil rights organizations, passed the 1991 Civil Rights and Women's Equity Act to overturn five particularly disastrous Supreme Court decisions. Yet, when one considers this institution's own internal affirmative action, the picture is disheartening. In Congress, African American staffers hold only 3.7% or 300 of the 8,200 high-level posts in a city—Washington, DC—that is overwhelmingly Black; Latinos hold 150 of these posts and Asian Americans, 45. And nearly half of these few work for Congress's 44 minority members. Worse, this sorry record is better than that of the high court and the White House.[7]

These same powerful forces in Washington often pontificate about "human rights" abroad while right here at home oppressed minorities are subjected to a heinous discrimination and the remedy—affirmative action—is blocked. At the same time, rampant cronyism that is objectively racist rules the roost in these circles. Ethnic minorities are told to work hard and allow merit to operate. Yet, a recent *Washington Post* article reveals what happens in reality. Air Force Generals have received promotion via a corrupt "secret system-within-a-system ... unknown to Congress or the secretary of defense for 30 years." In other words, merit was not the principle here but connections—a pattern repeated in elite circles throughout the nation.[8]

This tendency has been particularly evident in the much ballyhooed private sector. With all of its flaws, non-minority women and minorities have received a better shake from the public sector than the private sector. This is due in part to the fact that the public sector is more subject to democratic influence via the ballot box. Thus, a recent U.S. Labor Department study found that non-minority women and oppressed minorities are being excluded from corporate executive posts and face a "glass ceiling" that blocks their advancement. They are more likely to be placed in human resources and public relations jobs than in the sales or production posts are often the "fast track" to management. Said Lynn Martin, Secretary of Labor, "The glass ceiling ... deprives our economy of new leaders, new sources of creativity—the would-be pioneers of the business world. If our end game is to compete successfully in today's global market, then we have to unleash the full potential of the American work force."

This study focused on the *Fortune* 500 corporations, showed that they have neglected the most basic affirmative action tasks. When seeking executives, these companies neglect to make executive search firms aware of either their equal opportunity obligations as federal contractors or their desire that referrals be made from a diversified pool of applicants. Managers choose their successors, who tend to be individuals like themselves, i.e., Euro-American males. Employee performance evaluations are marked by bias: minority employees evaluated by non-minority male managers tend to have the poorest evaluations and women's evaluations often include such irrelevant terms as "happy" or "friendly" while white men generally are rated by performance.[9]

This damning report by the Labor Department allegedly was held up for several months by the White House, which was engaged in a bitter dispute over civil rights legislation that would bolster affirmative action. Yet this report objectively serves as reason why affirmative action should exist; for without strong laws and external pressure mandating affirmative action, ingrained patterns of discrimination tend to assert themselves.

This study also underscores the hypocrisy imbedded in the private sector. For while overpaid corporate executives moan about how affirmative action allegedly undermines merit, they do not raise such an outcry about the growing effort to force local governments to purchase exclusively from firms in their area, irrespective of "merit." This "local preference" has been backed widely though it is just another form of affirmative action and, in a sense, less justifiable. For example, the *New York Times* of 30 March 1992 reports that New York City in 1984 began favoring local companies in contracts for products ranging from police cars to software, as long as their bids are no more than 5% higher than competing bids from outsiders. Nassau County, New York has raised this limit to 10%. These local entities have ignored the outcry from the international community that such practices violate the General Agreement Against Tariffs and Trades. "Merit" has disappeared from the discourse of the private sector in this case.

Unfortunately, oppressed minorities and non-minority women not on the management track have faced a similar fate. A glimpse of how dire the situation is was provided by the General Accounting Office, Congress's investigative arm, which examined the operation in 16 states of the Job Training Partnership Act, which is supposed to train workers for skilled jobs. This $4 billion-a-year program pays companies a substantial part of workers' wages while they are being trained for jobs. Mostly this program has been yet another boondoggle for big business. In one unidentified project, the study said, 55% of the white men, who received instruction in electronics, obtained jobs that paid the "highest wages," an average of $7.50 an hour. But among the Black men only 26% received electronics training, while 42% received training in food services and health care at an average wage of less than $6 per hour. The study found that Blacks usually did not receive any training or on-the-job training and when they did, it was usually for lower-paying jobs. The study found "blatant racism and sexism" in the program. According to Franklin Frazier of the GAO, "Some employers (said) they didn't want them to send out a black or a Hispanic or a woman. And in some cases, whenever (projects) would send minorities to the employer, none of them would be hired." As a result, this heralded legislation wound up "training" many minority workers to work in fast food joints and as maids.[10]

This study is even more revealing, for the legislation authorizing the JTPA was promoted as the crowning accomplishment of then Senator Dan Quayle's legislative career and the most significant piece of legislation passed to this point to insure that minorities and non-minority women would have the skills to compete in the marketplace. What is revealed is that rampant discrimination persists and that affirmative action is needed more than ever. However, Vice President Quayle—despite his knowledge of these facts—has been one of the more adamant opponents of civil rights legislation and affirmative action.

Oppressed minorities and non-minority women are not only discriminated against when it comes to obtaining management posts and jobs as production workers; they face similar hurdles in the professions. In California, white males constitute 93% of the lawyers who have been in practice for over 20 years. Of those lawyers with 10-19 years experience, 27% of the white men earned less than $75,000, compared to 40% of the women and 42% of the racial and ethnic minorities. By contrast, 41% of the white men earned $125,000 or more, compared to 23% of the women and 19% of the minorities. Similar patterns obtain within the medical profession.[11]

The much heralded "mainstream media," the alleged guardian of the First Amendment, has been similarly culpable. The *Washington Post* of 16 April 1992 reported that the TV conglomerate ABC not only discriminated against its African American employees but that their counsel concealed evidence and deliberately misled the court. Management surreptitiously sent a management spy to a meeting of minority employees and engaged in other unsavory tactics to derail this suit. Unfortunately, such practices are all too typical of the media monopolies.

The discriminatory barriers that minorities and non-minority women encounter in finding work is one of the most persuasive arguments for the continuation—indeed, the escalation—of affirmative action. Though demagogues point to affirmative action as another form of burdensome government regulation, the record shows otherwise. The Executive Order issued by President Johnson and extended by President Nixon requires any

federal contractor with 50 or more employees or a federal contract worth more than $50,000 to adopt an affirmative action
plan. According to the Labor Department, more than 95,000
companies employing 27 million workers and having contracts
worth a total of $184 billion are covered by this federal pro-
gram. Pursuant to this program, companies are supposed to
strive to make their workforce match percentages of "qualified"
minorities and non-minority women in the local labor pool. Because so many private companies receive federal contracts, the
reach of affirmative action is broad. Yet, it is the public sector
that has been most responsive, which puts into question the
popularly repeated bromide that sees the private sector as the
savior of humankind.[12]

Income Redistribution

Yet, it is undeniable that the right wing was able to use the
shield of misrepresenting affirmative action to mask the redistribution of wealth from bottom to top that occurred with accel-
erated speed during the Reagan-Bush years. For too many in
the working class, this redistribution of wealth was *not* the
issue, but affirmative action *was*. However, although it has
been difficult to prove how affirmative action took a job from
anyone, proof is abundant that this wealth redistribution did
take place. According to *Business Week* of 18 November 1991,
"Median household income fell 1.7% in 1990 and the poverty
rate jumped 13.5%." As a result, the U.S. has had a "demand
short economy" that facilitates recession. According to the *New
York Times* of 5 March 1992, "an outsized 60 percent of the
growth in after-tax income of all American families between
1977 and 1989—and an even heftier three-fourths of the gain in
pretax income—went to the wealthiest 660,000 families, each of
which had an annual income of at least $310,000 a year for a
household of four ... the slice (of wealth) belonging to the top 1
percent grew to 13 percent of all family income, up from 9
percent ... the bottom 40 percent of families had actual declines
in income." This massive grand theft was confirmed by a study
issued by the Federal Reserve Board.[13]

This income redistribution was accompanied by a decline in
the overall standard of living. The UN Development Program
ranked the U.S. 7th in "human development" by employing an
index that combined per capita income with education and life

expectancy. This country was ranked 10th when it came to discrimination against women.[14]

Needless to say, these disastrous trends have impacted minorities and non-minority women most of all, in part because of the structural crisis that has hit U.S. industry. In 1970 the nation's steel plants employed 531,000 workers but by 1991 the figure had fallen to 185,000. In 1971 GM, Ford and Chrysler employed 848,000 workers but these numbers have declined significantly since then. General Motors alone closed 20 assembly plants between 1980 and 1990, though it has since opened plants in Eastern Europe. Nissan, Honda, Mazda and other Japanese corporations have opened plants in this country but have tended to site their facilities far from areas with large concentrations of African Americans, allegedly because of the latter's propensity toward trade union militancy. Many of the jobs eliminated by U.S. manufacturers were held by African Americans particularly; jobs remaining require an upgrading of skill. African Americans were 9.5% of the labor force in 1987 but received only 5.1% of training that would lead to higher-skilled, higher-paid jobs while Euro-Americans were 86% of the labor force and received 92.2% of such training, according to a recent study. This is even more unfortunate when it is considered that the state of Illinois alone will need 1,000 tool and die workers each year until the year 2000; 2,000 precision metal workers each year over the next decade, and 2,400 machine set operators per year over the same period. The attack on affirmative action and the aforementioned failure of the Job Training Partnership Act paints an especially dire picture for African American workers.[15]

Perversely, the bleaker the picture becomes for affirmative action recipients, the more the scapegoating of them for the nation's ills escalates. The fact that "Japan bashing" has proliferated simultaneously has given added energy to this racist scapegoating. Not surprisingly, Klanwatch—a project of the Southern Poverty Law Center—has noted that for the fourth consecutive year there has been a rise in hate-related violence and an increase the number of hate groups in this country.[16] Despite—or perhaps because of—this sickening spiral, other disturbing ideological trends have grown in unexpected circles. The "Black Conservative" movement has not grown necessarily though it has become influential—not least because of ceaseless promotion in the mass media. Their major issue has been opposition to affirmative action. Strikingly, Black capitalists have not been in the vanguard of those endorsing their program, perhaps because they recognize the importance of affirmative action in boosting their own position. Earl Graves, a leading African-American entrepreneur, in his magazine *Black Enterprise* repeatedly has excoriated "Black Conservatives."[17] Interestingly, those associated with this conservative grouping are disproportionately either academics like Shelby Steele or bureaucrats like Clarence Thomas, all on the government dole. More distressing is the fact that the progressive weekly, *In These Times*, in a 24 July 1991 editorial announced, "whatever the moral legitimacy and past benefits of affirmative action, this strategy is reaching a dead end, increasingly playing into the hands of the right." Unfortunately, the upsurge of the right wing has caused a vacillation in certain circles.

Anti-Affirmative Action Ploys

Simultaneously severe flaws in the anti-affirmative action discourse have been papered over. There is the idea popularized by some that affirmative action recipients are stigmatized and suffer a loss of self-esteem. As noted by Dr. Richard Hudson of Mercy College, "... we are never given empirical data or studies to support the thesis.... Support for the thesis relies on selective anecdotal evidence."[18] To the contrary, oppressed minorities and non-minority women are of the opinion that they have to be "twice as good to get half as far."

Then there is the question of quotas. There seems to be no outcry against the quotas that served to exclude minorities and non-minority women, which made affirmative action a dire necessity. Similarly, there seems to be no outcry against the quotas that have impacted favorably certain groups; quotas that have kept women out of many jobs were de facto quotas favoring men.

Moreover, the issue of how quotas allegedly override merit does not arise when one considers import quotas on machine tools or Japanese cars. Strikingly, these quotas, too have an ethnic bias in that machine tools from Switzerland, Germany, Britain and like nations are exempt from quotas while Taiwan and Japan are the main nations affected.[19] Likewise, quotas were used in immigration laws for decades to favor certain European nations and to bar Asians, Africans and Latin Americans; this policy did not change until 1965.

Affirmative action is necessary to override ingrained biases and institutionalized discrimination. It is well known that connections replace competition in the search for employment; this is disadvantageous for affirmative action recipients. Yet, the Seventh Circuit Court of Appeals in *EEOC v. Chicago Miniature Lamp Works* ruled recently that though racial discrimination "remains widespread in Chicago," a North Side factory did not violate 1964 Civil Rights Act by relying on "word-of-mouth" for filling entry-level jobs, even though this negatively impacted African-Americans. "Connections replacing competition" has been sanctified in law.[20]

Because affirmative action has been portrayed by demagogues as the source of all evil, many have retreated to the idea that "race specific" remedies (somehow the idea of "gender specific" remedies is not noted in this context) should be jettisoned in favor of "universal" programs. The prominent sociologist William Julius Wilson has suggested such; however, this elides the fact that the ill—racial bias—is "race specific", which suggests that the remedy should be specific to the ill. Moreover, Prof. Charles V. Willie of Harvard has pointed out that "the universal approach advocated by Mr. Wilson and others also has not worked for black students in federal student aid programs." There can be racial bias in the administering of "universal" programs. This is why those who point to national health care as the ideal "universal" program that obviates the need for "race specific" remedies neglect the point that studies show bias in the area of organ transplants and other areas of health care.[21]

Another canard often repeated is the idea that race- based affirmative action particularly (again, there is this idea that African Americans are the sole beneficiary) overlooks the class dimension. Prof. Martin Kilson of Harvard has analogized German reparations after the Holocaust: "Compensatory responses to Jewish survivors ... have been quite broadcast ... even with the state of Israel (itself not existing at time of injury) functioning in part as beneficiary. So just as Nazi coercion of Jews affected all German Jews ... American slavery and racial-caste victimization affected all Afro-Americans, not just working class and poor, and this in turn requires that the compensatory policy—affirmative action policy—likewise benefit all black Americans." Prof. Kilson also has objected to the idea that some Euro-Americans are being made to pay for the "sins" of their ancestors or for "sins" they did not commit. He observes that "the taxes of Germans in general correctly pay reparations to injured [Jews]." This approach, he argues, has a "good legal pedigree—namely successor rulers and citizenry to a state deemed victimizers of others ... also succeed to indemnitory obligations, whether or not [they] themselves were direct victimizers." He points out finally that affirmative action policy has been practiced in behalf of "farmers, veterans, businesses ... regions (e.g., Tennessee River Valley)" and such individuals as black lung victims, not to mention "contracts and jobs allocated by white ethnic-bloc political machines."[22]

These are not the only flaws in the anti-affirmative action discourse. Take the question of testing, for example. Tests are important, not only for admission into colleges but also to receive certain jobs, e.g., civil service posts. Yet numerous studies have pointed to the biases inherent in many of these tests. The National Center for Fair and Open Testing has shown that commercial coaching courses that train students to take standardized tests can raise scores significantly; these courses can cost over $500. Moreover, these tests use questions with terms and ideas like dividends, deeds and heirlooms that those from low-income families are unlikely to know. Furthermore, recent reports indicate that some have gained improper and illegal access to answers to tests, e.g., recent Boston civil service tests and the Scholastic Aptitude and Achievement tests. It is unclear how widespread such practices are but certainly this raises questions about the propriety of using such tests to screen out affirmative action recipients.[23]

There are other problems with tests. Some studies show that many of them are biased against girls and women. Young women traditionally score lower on college entrance exams even though they make better grades in high school. Multiple choice tests have been criticized as not presenting a whole picture of aptitude or intelligence. Critics also charge that scoring is subject to human bias.[24]

Despite all of these problems with tests, the major issue focused on by opponents of affirmative action is the practice of "race norming"—or adjusting employment test scores by race to improve ethnic minorities' job prospects. For the past 45 years, many state employment agencies have used a test known as the General Aptitude Test Battery to refer job applicants to public and private employers; the test measures areas as diverse as reading comprehension and manual dexterity. African Americans and Latinos have tended to do less well than others and have as a result received fewer job referrals. Yet many who do get jobs perform better than their test scores would indicate; hence, in 1981 the Labor Department decided to adjust scores by race. During the debate over the 1991 Civil Rights and Women's Equity Act, "race norming" became an issue manipulated by the right wing, though they expressed less concern about flawed tests that evidently did not correlate effectively with adequate job performance. Typically, in December 1991 the Bush Administration moved to bar race norming—a form of affirmative action—but took no steps to correct flawed tests that made the practice necessary. The Administration action applied to tests taken by 600,000 per year in 30 states; thus, minorities were left in a worse condition.[25]

While the Bush Administration had no hesitation in continuing the use of discriminatory tests, they have taken a different view when it comes to the use of undercover tests to root out discrimination in employment, housing and business. Clandestine testers help to document the existence of discrimination, which often goes undetected. The technique generally involves sending people alike in virtually every way except ethnicity to, for example, apply for jobs, housing or mortgages. The results often reveal that non-minorities receive preferential treatment— contrary to right-wing opinion. Nevertheless, only the Department of Housing and Urban Development, among federal agencies, provides money for the use of clandestine testers to enforce anti-discrimination statutes or to study the extent of discrimination. Thus, the Administration not only opposes affirmative action but has refused to use a reliable tool that reveals the bias that makes affirmative action so necessary.[26]

Upsurge of Racism

Given this assault on all fronts—relaxation of affirmative action measures, attacking anti-discrimination statutes, the escalation of hate crimes, etc.—it should not be deemed surprising that an upsurge in racism and sexism has been detected. Of course, this assault has been met by a determined resistance. The National Alliance Against Racist and Political Repression has won victories, as has the NAACP, the Southern Poverty Law Center, etc. Nevertheless, it is useful to survey the landscape so as to assess what obstacles remain to overcome. In part because of the decline in use of clandestine testers, a recent study showed that African Americans and Latinos face bias more than half the time they tried to rent or buy homes in 25 metropolitan areas. This kind of housing bias correlates with employment in that new jobs increasingly are migrating to suburbs inaccessible to oppressed minorities.[27]

Because of deteriorating socioeconomic conditions in the neighborhoods where they are consigned, African Americans and Latinos are more likely to be crime victims, according to the National Crime Victimization Survey released by the Bureau of Justice Statistics. For example, there were 13 robberies for every 1000 Black residents in 1990, compared to 4.5 for whites and 13.9 for Latinos.[28]

The bias continues inside prison. African American and Latino inmates at Elmira prison in New York regularly face discrimination in discipline, job assignments and housing. Eighty percent of New York state inmates are oppressed minority. The harsher discipline they face often results in their spending longer terms in prison. Elmira prison was investigated initially in 1984 when it was reported that Ku Klux Klan activities were taking place there. State courts prevented the dismissal of a prison official who was a KKK member. Unfortunately, the pattern at Elmira is seen nationwide.[29]

It is well to recognize that this kind of bias is impossible to localize solely against African Americans and Latinos or Asian Americans and Native Americans. Anti-Semitism has been on the upswing lately. Recent reports suggest that anti-Catholic bias—a major scourge of the 1920s—has returned with a vengeance.[30] A recent study has shown that the same powerful forces who are ultimately responsible for blocking the progress of affirmative action—the monopoly capitalist class—have played a role in fomenting difficulties between African Americans and Jewish Americans.[31]

Though there has been a decline in certain overt racist attitudes over the past 45 years, recent studies compel one to view this development with caution. Prof. Howard Schuman of Survey Research Center of the University of Michigan has pointed out that "... when white Americans say they favor integrated schools or neighborhoods, what they really mean is a few Black students or families in a predominantly white environment." Prof. Reynolds Farley of the same school has noted that "white respondents tended to prefer neighborhoods that were integrated in the sense of one Black house out of a total of 15 (about 6 percent), while Black respondents were much more likely to prefer integration in the sense of 50/50 white and Black."[32]

Education and Affirmative Action

Affirmative action is one tool used to slice this ugly gordian knot. Bias prevents ethnic minorities from obtaining jobs; affirmative action is the antidote. Affirmative action in the field of education is particularly crucial in that diplomas, certificates and learning are necessary for many of the jobs that will be created by the year 2000. However, because of bias and housing discrimination, minorities being able to obtain education becomes problematic. This hostile bias has encouraged many minorities, particularly African Americans, to disdain the very notion of desegregation of education. Yet, in a brief filed in a recent Supreme Court case, signed by 58 leading scholars and summarizing research over the last 20 years, it was noted: that desegregation of schools is associated with moderate academic gains for minorities with no harm to white students (this is due in part to the fact that non-minority schools tend to have more resources); that desegregation plans work best when they cover as many grades as possible when they encompass as large a geographic area as possible, and when they stick to clearly defined goals over the long haul; and that school desegregation can positively influence residential integration.[33]

The working class of the future is now in elementary school and the record shows that these students increasingly are oppressed minority. This suggests that if these students are consigned to inferior schools, not only will minorities and the working class as a whole suffer, but the economy as a whole. For by 1995 conservative estimates indicate that 1/3 of U.S. public school students will be minorities. Simultaneously a recent study by People for the American Way finds young people exceedingly pessimistic about race relations. Many of the non-minority youth were adamantly opposed to affirmative action, viewing it as a form of bias against them.[34]

Affirmative steps need to be taken to guarantee that inferior education for oppressed minorities ceases. But discrimination has become so pervasive that recently a group of African American and Latino parents sued the school system of Alexandria, Virginia, alleging that the selection process for a popular all-day kindergarten program is discriminatory.[35] Bias does not exempt 5-year-olds!

But bias does not stop there. The Middle States Association of Colleges and Schools which provides accreditation for educational institutions has included a "diversity" requirement to prod schools to engage in affirmative action to diversify their student body, staff and faculty. Yet, the Bush Administration has railed against this small step and has sought to bar this move. Similarly, in 1990 the U.S. Education Department issued a surprise declaration that minority scholarships were illegal and discriminated against non-minority students. This ignited a fightback by groups representing virtually all of the nation's 3,400 colleges and universities, in part because during the 1980s the percentage of bachelor's degrees awarded to African Americans dropped from 6.5% to 5.7% and the percentage of doctoral degrees dropped from 5.8% to 4.6%. As is typical in such instances, the Administration sought to paint these scholarships as a "Black Issue" while ignoring that there are special scholarships for Armenian students, Jewish students, etc. This fightback forced the Administration to retreat but their actions in this area still left more than a residue of confusion and anger.[36]

Though the right wing has complained about oppressed minorities and non-minority women "taking over" campuses, actually their numbers remain quite small on faculties. When these groups go to court in complaint against discrimination, they fare poorly; indeed, the group that fares best in pursuing such employment discrimination claims are white males litigating against historically Black institutions. The pattern at the University of California--Berkeley is indicative of trends elsewhere. Among senior faculty there, non-minority women, African American and Native American faculty earn lower salaries on average than white men of their same rank, even when their experience, field, type and degree and kind of employment are considered.[37]

The academy has been one of the few institutions where the Red Scare and McCarthyism did not totally rout progressive forces. Moreover, the academy is infused yearly with droves of questioning students who have not accepted the shibboleths of bourgeois society. In a real sense the future of the country is being decided in educational institutions. In addition the academy, unlike many workplaces, contains unions that are not totally powerless. As a result, the academy has been a crucial battleground in the struggle for affirmative action. This helps to explain why some of the staunchest critics of affirmative action—Shelby Steele, Paul Hollander, Allan Bloom, et al— come from the campuses.

Therefore, if the campuses can emerge as benighted bastions of opposition to affirmative action, it suggests the uphill climb that advocates of equity face elsewhere. Yet so much disinformation clouds the debate, it is not surprising that affirmative action has faced difficulties. For example, a Louis Harris poll in June 1991 asked a sample of adults, "Do you favor or oppose federal laws requiring affirmative action programs for women and minorities in employment and education provided there are not rigid quotas?" The results: 75% were in favor, including 71% of whites and 93% of Blacks. Now consider a *Wall Street Journal*/NBC News poll done a month earlier asking: "All in all, do you favor or oppose affirmative action programs in business for blacks and other minority groups?" Note the question did not mention women. And it produced a much narrower 57% to 33% margin or approval, with 86% of Blacks but only 52% of whites approving. This underscores the "Afro-phobia," the resentment and hatred of African Americans, which has been so useful over the years to the right wing. A Gallup poll in April 1991 asked, "Are quotas necessary to accomplish fairness in education, hiring and promotion?" Blacks said yes by a 61% to 26% margin, while whites opposed 59% to 29%. Another apparently inflammatory term is "racial preference." The same Gallup survey asked, "Because of past discrimination should qualified blacks receive preference over equally qualified whites in such matters as getting into college or getting jobs?" Whites answered negatively 72% to 19% and even Blacks split with 48% saying yes and 42% no.[38]

What is even more striking is the inadequacy, distortion and racial polarization embodied in such questions. The last question particularly is loaded and warps the notion of affirmative action which, after all, includes half of what are considered to be "white people," i.e., women. The point that "preference" along with "quota" are inadequate to describe affirmative action should also be mentioned. But above all, one notices the repeated use of "Afro-phobia" built up over centuries of slavery and decades of racism to deflect attention from the real meaning of affirmative action. This is the meaning of questions that place affirmative action solely within a "black-white" context, which distorts woefully a program that includes a significant percentage of white beneficiaries.

The Significance of *Weber*

Perhaps we should not be surprised that the bourgeois press would seek to inflame and distort the debate on this crucial public policy question. Unfortunately, from the time it exploded in public consciousness, affirmative action has been cloaked in canards. Take the facts behind the important U.S. Supreme Court ruling, *United Steelworkers of America v. Weber.* There is a Kaiser Aluminum plant in Gramercy, Louisiana, 25 miles north of New Orleans. Brian Weber, son of a grocer, had grown up in Reserve, not far from there. It was a Jim Crow town with railroad tracks separating the white from the "other" side of town.

Weber sought work in the Kaiser plant. Part of the plant made chlorine, another part produced alumina powder from Jamaican bauxite. Weber, who is white, and Kernell Goudia, who is Black, began work there in 1968. Because of past discrimination, in 1969 Kaiser began hiring Blacks and whites at a 50-50 rate into the plant, so that the plant could reflect ultimately the relevant labor pool which was 39% African American. (Note that this 50-50 selection process was a de facto quota.) However, there were certain skilled jobs—electrician, insulator, welder—that required certain skills. African Americans had been denied training for such posts because of racism. Kaiser and the union worked out a program of affirmative action to overcome this hurdle. However, to become part of the list eligible for this training, it was decided there would be two separate seniority lists to draw from—one Black, one white. This overrode certain seniority advantages enjoyed by some white workers. Brian Weber sued. In 1979 the Supreme Court decided the case. He lost.[39]

This was just before the election of Ronald Reagan and perhaps serves to explain why the bourgeois press did not stress that the high court had placed their imprimatur on a reviled "quota." Also unemphasized was the fact that the "quota" was the result of collective bargaining between labor and management. Also unstressed was that this 50-50 program helped to insure that the whites selected for training would be selected not because of a positive relationship with a foreman but due to more objective standards.

Substantial distortion has been the sad fate of affirmative action to this point. The role of unions in pushing for such programs has been shrouded. Buzz words like "reverse discrimination"—the key phrase used in most articles on the Weber case—have proliferated. The ugly bigotry that makes affirmative action necessary has been overlooked. The benefits of affirmative action for its recipients and for the health of the economy have been ignored. This is a horrible distortion, but particularly so when one considers the African American population.

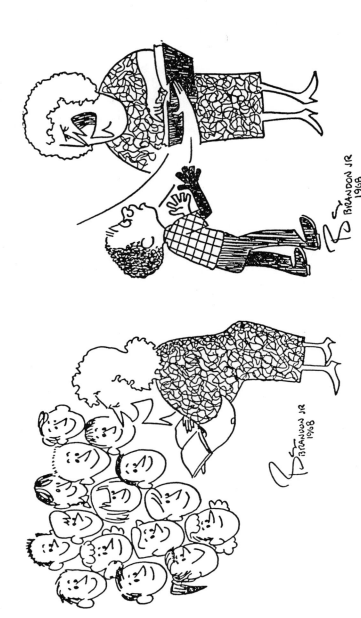

"—AND IN 1954 A SUPREME COURT DECISION PUT AN END TO SEGREGATION IN ALL OUR SCHOOLS!"

"THE 250 YEARS OF NEGRO SLAVERY IS IN THERE... GIVE ME THAT BOOK ...HERE IT IS, THIS PARAGRAPH TELLS THE ENTIRE STORY!"

2.

African Americans &
Affirmative Action

There is little question that African Americans have been in the vanguard of the struggle for affirmative action, especially Black workers. After all, those who feel the most pain scream the loudest. In other words, the objective position of Black workers particularly predisposes them to pursue measures of benefit to the most oppressed sectors of the class and, therefore, the working class as a whole. Because of African American vigilance on this crucial front, opponents of equity have sought to paint affirmative action as a "black issue" alone, neglecting that sizeable numbers of non-Blacks benefit from this program. They seek to play on and heighten deep-seated anti-Black attitudes lurking close to the surface of U.S. society and promoted zealously by certain sectors of the ruling elite.

Nevertheless, this demagogy should not cause us to ignore the fact that the African American community is in dire need of affirmative action precisely because it is a prime recipient of bigotry in virtually all realms of U.S. society. Some of the forms of discrimination that we thought had disappeared during the 1960s are still with us. For example, a recent study by Professors Verna M. Keith and Cedric Herring that appeared in the November 1991 edition of the *American Journal of Sociology* suggests that African Americans with the darkest skin tone continue to experience severe economic and occupational disadvantages when compared to their lighter skinned Black brethren. It was thought that the "black is beautiful" movement of the 1960s had eroded this ante-bellum vestige. Yet, after investigation, these scholars concluded that "the fairer one's pigmentation, the higher his or her occupational standing." Similarly, an African American with a lighter complexion has on average a 50 percent higher income than one with a dark complexion. Certainly questions could be raised about this study—especially in defining what is "dark" and what is "light"—but the point is that backward and ugly forms of discrimination that some had thought had disappeared so that we could move on to tackle more sophisticated forms of bigotry, continue to linger.[1]

At times in the African American community the idea is rumored that things are worse now than during the darkest days of the 1950s. Given the erosion of Jim Crow, this could easily be seen as inflated rhetoric. Yet, when one considers recent revelations, it is easy to see why such ideas are heard. For example, according to the *Los Angeles Times* of 3 October 1991, there are still establishments in the South that have separate entrances and services for Black and non-Black customers. For example, "Pete's Out in the Cold Bar" in New Orleans and in "nearly a dozen other mostly blue-collar, family-run lounges throughout New Orleans, the customs of yesterday still thrive today—blacks and whites eat and drink in separate quarters;" i.e., the process of desegregation has not been concluded despite the plain language of the Civil Rights Act of 1964. It is equally well known that some doctors in the Deep South persist in the practice of segregating their waiting rooms. In other words, African Americans are still regarded as hewers of wood and drawers of water and affirmative action becomes even more of a pressing necessity.

It would be mistaken, however, to view racism as a question merely for the Deep South. Three recently published studies outline the dimensions of the problem. The Chicago Urban League's study, *The Geography of Opportunity*, describes the wide racial disparities existing in the Chicago area's employment market. Jobs continue to flee the city, where many African Americans live, to suburban areas where generally they do not live. The report also challenges the prevailing affirmative action myth that equal opportunity initiatives have triumphed and that racial differences in job access have been removed, particularly in the suburbs and high-paying jobs.

The Leadership Council for Metropolitan Open Communities' Research draws a direct connection between suburban housing discrimination against African Americans and the astoundingly high levels of unemployment within Black communities. More damning is the report issued by the Brookings Institution which shows that senior executives continue to discriminate illegally against African Americans in hiring and promotion. Added together these reports argue convincingly for heightened affirmative action, for there are institutionalized and structural barriers to equal opportunity that only affirmative action can address.[2]

Just as racism is not a problem just for the deep South, it is not an issue just for the Midwest either. According to the Beverly Hills/Hollywood chapter of the NAACP, racial and sexual discrimination complaints filed with their office are up 45% in the past year. One African American woman employed by "'one of Hollywood's most successful independent production companies'" found a stuffed monkey with a noose around its neck hanging above her desk. "'One individual was told his skin color was too dark to work in one of the studio's executive buildings.'" The verdict in the Rodney King beating case exploded whatever was left of the myth that Southern California was some sort of racial paradise. The entertainment industry, one of the few U.S. industries that can compete successfully abroad, has proven to be one of the industries most in need of affirmative action.[3]

These broad patterns of discrimination have hit both male and female. However, there has been a tendency of late to stress the special crisis of African American men. This is understandable though it should not be interpreted to suggest that Black women are somehow doing well. Nonetheless, the figures are stunning. Forty percent of all adult Black males are functionally illiterate. More Black men between the ages of 15 and 44 are in jail or on probation than in college. Homicide is the leading cause of death among Black males 15 to 44 years of age. Their official unemployment rate of 12.6% exceeds the 6.8% jobless rate for the nation and the 10.9% rate for Black women. Over the last two decades, earnings of all men without college degrees have eroded, but Black men have lost more than any other group. Forty-three percent of Black men were married in 1974; 24% in 1990. The deindustrialization of the U.S. economy—the growth of "runaway shops" to South Korea and South Africa and the inability of U.S. companies to compete because of poor management and investment decisions—has hit Black male workers particularly hard. One can safely say that if affirmative action steps are not taken soon and vigorously, the idea of the Black man as an endangered species will become reality rather than slogan.[4]

However, not just Black male workers are suffering. More than a decade of Reagan-Bush policies have impoverished the African American community, male and female alike. The U.S. Census Bureau has reported that the number of poor African Americans has increased from 9.3 million to 9.8 million while their poverty rate remained unchanged at 31.9% from 1989 to 1990.[5] Such studies and figures suggest that race is not declining as a factor in U.S. life and that race-specific remedies like affirmative action are needed more than ever.

Despite this clear and convincing evidence, the right wing has been able to convince all too many that the massive redistribution of wealth from bottom to top that rocked the 1980s is not the source of the working class's problems. The problem, we are told, is that affirmative action means unqualified African Americans receive "racial preference" and "quotas" in order to receive benefits and jobs that should have gone to more deserving Euro-Americans.

Studies Prove Racism

Fortunately, of late a number of studies flatly refute such nonsense and demonstrate that virulent racism remains a major factor in U.S. life. On 26 September 1991, the ABC-TV program "Prime Time Live" used hidden cameras to demonstrate this simple fact. Correspondent Diane Sawyer travelled to St. Louis with two 28-year-old men, Glenn Brewer, an African American and John Kuhnen, who is white. They were assigned to shop in the same stores, try to rent the same apartments and apply for the same job. At several stores, Kuhnen gets instant service while Brewer is ignored—except for a salesman who kept a close eye on him. When they go for walks, a police car passes Kuhnen but slows down to give Brewer a once-over. At a car dealership, Kuhnen is offered a lower price and better financing than Brewer. Inquiring about a job at a dry cleaner that has advertised for help, Kuhnen is told jobs are still available while Brewer is told, "The positions are taken." Following up a "for rent" sign, Kuhnen is promptly offered an apartment, which he does not take; 10 minutes later Brewer is told it had been rented for hours. This television program presented a devastating portrait of contemporary racism and inferentially a persuasive argument why affirmative action is needed to overcome barriers that block the path toward equal opportunity.[6]

Evidence that this was not some staged photo opportunity was provided subsequently by another TV station, this time KSTP-TV in Minneapolis. As reported in the March-April 1992 *Columbia Journalism Review*, reporter Joel Glover conducted a four-month undercover investigation. It showed security guards at such stores as Carson Pirie Scott and K-Mart systematically (and illegally) targeting Black customers as potential shoplifters—despite the fact that as the store's own internal records as well as national statistics indicate, most shoplifters are white. Outraged by this program, African Americans and their allies organized a credit-card-cutting, button-wearing "I'm Not a Shoplifter" boycott. Chagrined Carson instituted changes in all 13 of its area stores, including hiring more minority security guards, providing racial sensitivity courses for all employees and engaging an outside organization to monitor the store's treatment of minorities. Some thirty other retailers are developing similar programs under the guidance of the Minneapolis Downtown Council. This is an indication of how mass protest can enforce and initiate affirmative action irrespective of the torpor of courts, legislatures, bosses or even unions.

Opponents of affirmative action persist in stating that African Americans are receiving dispensations and benefits denied to others. One would think that African Americans receive certain advantages when applying for jobs, but reality does not dovetail with this assertion.

The ABC-TV program substantiates this and a recent study by the Urban Institute goes even further. Despite the inflamed rhetoric surrounding affirmative action, their study, published as *Opportunities Denied, Opportunities Diminished: Racial Discrimination in Hiring*, was the first attempt to measure directly differential treatment of white and Black job seekers applying for entry-level posts. A total of 476 hiring audits were conducted in Washington, DC and Chicago during the summer of 1990. Ten pairs of young men—one Black, one white—were matched carefully on all characteristics that could affect a hiring decision. They applied for entry-level jobs advertised in the newspaper, and reported their treatment at every stage of the hiring process. The process demonstrated that unequal treatment of African American job seekers is entrenched and widespread. In one out of five audits, the white applicant was able to advance farther through the hiring process than his Black counterpart. In one of out of eight audits, the white was offered a job although his equally qualified Black partner was not. The authors conclude, "The results also contradict the view that reverse discrimination is commonplace."

The details of this study—the first to analyze the alleged existence of "reverse discrimination"—are bracing. Black applicants were questioned about qualifications even before being given an application form; whites were not. Blacks were more likely to be given brief job interviews. Whites were more likely to receive encouraging comments during interviews. Blacks were more likely to encounter unfavorable treatment in higher paying, higher status jobs and in jobs involving substantial customer contact. Blacks were more likely to encounter unfavorable treatment from white employers than from minority employers. Blacks were more likely to encounter unfavorable treatment when they applied for jobs in predominantly white neighborhoods (this is yet another argument for residential desegregation).

The results of this study suggest why advocates of the "reverse discrimination" thesis are considered demagogues. Without a shred of evidence an incendiary "reverse discrimination" charge is tossed into the arena of public debate. Another study, by Kathryn M. Nickerman and Joleen Kirschenman of the University of Chicago, also refutes this spurious claim. Interviews with senior executives at 185 Chicago-area firms concluded that employers did not hesitate to use race stereotypes to evaluate the quality of workers. When talking about African Americans, Euro-Americans interviewed for the study made comments such as: "The quality of (Blacks') education is not as great as white folks' from the suburbs," or complained that they had "bad experiences in that sector." The researchers warned that this type of behavior resulted in biased job performance ratings, steering Black job applicants toward certain jobs and limiting Blacks' access to on-the-job training.

There are still other studies that conclusively rebut the mendacious claim of "reverse discrimination" and show that what this nation needs to focus on is *how to reverse discrimination.* In January 1991 the National Opinion Research Center of the University of Chicago released "Ethnic Images," a study on racial tolerance in the United States. Authored by Tom W. Smith and James A. Davis, the study revealed that nationwide, whites by and large still believe that Blacks are viewed as lazier, less intelligent, less patriotic and more prone to violence than several other ethnic groups. Needless to say, these ideas do not remain dormant but are acted on. *The National Law Journal* recently conducted a survey to determine worker perceptions of discrimination in employment. The 1990 random survey of 803 adults revealed that 51% (48% of whites and 64% of Blacks) felt employers practice some form of discrimination in hiring and promotion. In addition, 5% of whites and 25% of Blacks believed that they had experienced racial discrimination; and 23% of whites and 36% of Blacks felt were they were discriminated against for other reasons.

Commenting on this evidence, Prof. Alvin Poussaint of Harvard Medical School concluded that "the burden of proof is on Black people to prove that they are competent." He went on to add that employers focus unduly on racial stereotypes when making decisions in the workplace. Prof. Rhett Jones of Brown university added, "The guy from Howard [University] can be very smart, but he won't even be able to get in the door." Nor is a degree from Harvard a guarantee of equal treatment.[7]

Taken as a whole, these studies are a powerful argument for the existence and expansion of affirmative action. If employers are forced to have goals and timetables mandating the number of African Americans that are supposed to be on the payroll, it serves to mitigate the poisonous impact of racist stereotypes. Indeed, these studies argue for quotas, precisely because of the toxic and pervasive impact of these stereotypes; flexible goals would allow employers to go through the motions of affirmative action while allowing their racism to blunt the implementation of equity.

Racism and Black Class Divisions

Though racism is a multi-class phenomenon hitting all classes and sectors of the African American community, recent studies also suggest that economic fissures are developing in this community that could have significant implications. According to a recent study by the Population Reference Bureau, the number of African Americans defined as affluent has doubled since the 1960s, but Blacks at the bottom of the income ladder have made little progress, with one-third still mired in poverty. Given the pernicious impact of racism, the study comes to conclusions that could be questioned but certainly cannot be ignored. To wit, "the middle class blacks of the future may feel little in common with poor blacks because their experiences will have been dramatically different in so many ways." Yet, this point does shed light on the possible proliferation of the Clarence Thomas phenomenon. However, this point complicates but does not remove the need for affirmative action because even these ill-defined "middle class Blacks" will be subjected to racism, even if some lean toward neo-conservatism and just like Clarence Thomas, they receive affirmative action. Nor does the growth of class stratification among African-Americans necessarily augur a "declining significance of race." For racism remains quite useful even against "middle class Blacks," though admittedly this sector might be more predisposed than the Black working class to be seduced by the siren song of neo-conservatism.[8]

The point that has to be guarded against is that it seems that certain elite institutions have been more enthusiastic about affirmative action than their progressive counterparts. Albeit this may not be saying too much; yet, it is chilling to contemplate that the Joint Chiefs of Staff of the U.S. military may be hiring its *second* African American leader before the Institute of Policy Studies or *Mother Jones* magazine or *The Nation* hire their first.

In any case, arguably much too much is made of the so-called "Black middle class." First of all, this group is ill-defined to the point where in fact it often seems what is being discussed is a sector of the working class. Secondly, this sector is not representative of the Black community as a whole—unless one is misusing the term as a synonym for working class. More relevant for a discussion of the need for affirmative action is the structural crisis of U.S. capitalism that has led to a downsizing of the industrial base. According to the Labor Department's *Monthly Labor Review*, when jobs are lost because an employer goes out of business or a plant closes, African Americans tend to suffer more than others. The study looked at a sample of workers who had held jobs for at least three years and then lost them in the period 1979-1986—not through temporary layoffs, but through permanent plant shutdowns, company closures and structural changes. Study author Lori Kletzer of Williams College averred: "Black workers bore a relatively heavier burden of widespread job displacement during the 1980s because of the industries and occupations in which they were concentrated; they were also less likely to be reemployed and were out of work longer."[9] By inference one can conclude that whatever gains in employment were made via affirmative action in industry are now falling victim to the recession and the structural crisis. This raises the point of whether affirmative action should be given a higher priority at all levels—hiring, promotion and, if need be, layoffs.[9]

The "last hired, first fired" principle and the recession combined with the malevolent operation of racist stereotypes has led to a decimation of the Black component of the working class. Moreover, though the growth of the ill-defined "Black middle class" has been ballyhooed, receiving less attention has been how it, too, has been hit by the recent wave of corporate layoffs. According to Derryl L. Reed, president of the Black MBA Association, "Ten years ago, a company might have had the objective of increasing the black presence in its labor force to 10 percent, but that is not considered important any more.... And when it is time to cut costs, black professionals get the brunt of it because there generally is no access to the decision makers. We're not a part of the good old boy network." Mart T. Standard of the Association agreed. He was laid off and added, "Nearly every black person that I knew in the company got laid off. It seemed that black people were fairly new to the company and everyone got downgraded in the downsizing. Middle managers were placed in the field, and those who were in the field were placed out the door."[10]

Public Sector Jobs

Though castigated by the ultra-right, there is little doubt that African Americans have received a better shake from the public sector when compared to the private sector. Yet, the Reagan-Bush years have led to an all-out assault on the public sector that has hit Black workers particularly hard. In Chicago, for example, 1,000 city workers were laid off on 1 January 1992 alone. Said the *New York Times* of 10 December 1991, "The Ronald Reagan and Bush Administrations have helped create an atmosphere of such hostility toward affirmative action that government officials may feel that they can reduce the opportunities for blacks, at least at the Federal level."

The popular film "Hollywood Shuffle" captured the importance of the public sector for Black workers when the movie's hero was advised that if he could not make it as an actor he could always get a job at the Post Office. For the longest time, the public sector was a familiar redoubt for those few African Americans who graduated from college. But as a result of this traditional reliance, the conservative attack on this sector has had an especially devastating impact on African Americans. Baltimore, for example, has reduced its work force by 1,037 since July 1989. Bridgeport has laid off about 500 of its 4,200 workers and cut another 200 or so jobs through attrition over the past two years. And Detroit laid off 502 of its 19,500 employees in April, 300 of them police officers; roughly two-thirds of the officers were African American and that pattern of layoffs has been duplicated nationwide. In the 1991 and 1992 fiscal years, New York City has laid off or planned to lay off about 5,000 of its 234,000 workers and at least half of those laid off were either African American or Latino.

Roberta Lynch, director of public policy for the American Federation of State, County and Municipal Employees in Chicago has lamented: "The layoffs are almost certain to have a disproportionate impact on the minority community because the public sector has a greater concentration of [minorities].... Even if minorities and whites were to lose their jobs in equal numbers it would have a bigger impact in the minority community than it would in the white." Roger Wilkins of George Mason University hinted at why the assault on the public sector has been especially harmful for African Americans, "Private employers deem themselves responsible to only the market place. But public employers are responsible to the public. They have more pressures on them to be fair."[11]

As usual, African Americans have not accepted this situation without complaint. The NAACP particularly has been conducting an ongoing struggle against discrimination in the public sector. Not only have they struggled against the patterns of layoffs but its complement, mostly white suburbs discriminating against African Americans. The Association sued seven municipalities in New Jersey, charging that their resident-only employment policies locked out African Americans and other minorities. Thus, a pattern has developed: big cities where African Americans reside—Baltimore, Chicago, New York—are forced into layoffs, while mostly white suburbs that may be enjoying a bit more economic growth, effectively bar African Americans via residence requirements. Through the operation of this whipsaw between city and suburb, the public sector is losing its reputation for giving African Americans economic opportunity, while the private sector continues its traditional policy of discrimination. To break this logjam of bias, vigorous affirmative action is required; not pursuing such a policy is an alternative too ghastly to contemplate.[12]

One of the few growth sectors of the economy has been the military sector. Private companies like McDonnell-Douglas, Martin Marietta, General Dynamics—i.e., the military-industrial complex—have been fed trillions of tax dollars to make weapons so that the diktat of transnationals can be enforced worldwide. Not surprisingly, a notably virulent form of racism is found in these corporations. A group of African Americans workers at Lockheed are representative of what is going on in this "private-public" sector. These workers in Sunnyvale, California have complained of blatant racism on the job, from having KKK written on their time cards to being the object of racial slurs. The allegations came three months after a jury awarded $925,000 to Norman Drake, a Black Lockheed worker, who complained of similar harassment, including from a supervisor who used racial insults.[13]

In 1988 the FBI was obligated to settle a massive suit brought by Latino agents. This repressive sector has been no friend of African Americans. According to the 22 April 1992

Washington Post, African Americans, who constitute 5% of the roughly 10,000 agents "alleged they were being passed over for promotion, given lower bonuses, evaluated more harshly, subjected to more disciplinary inquiries and denied choice assignments." The suit was settled to the Black agents' satisfaction though few would claim that the problem of racism has been eliminated within this historic bastion of bigotry.

The attack on affirmative action in the public sector has been particularly devastating for African Americans. African Americans also have been told that the U.S. military, like the Post Office, could serve as the basis for a career. Sensitive to the image of imperialism abroad, U.S. rulers have been more aware than the private sector of this public relations question of integration. The effort to desegregate the military emerged six years before *Brown v. Board of Education.* Yet, any idea that the military has been a stronghold of affirmative action should have been disabused after the Chair of the U.S. Civil Rights Commission returned from a tour of U.S. military bases in Germany. Arthur Fletcher described pervasive race discrimination against African American service personnel and civilian employees in the armed forces. This racism extended from job evaluations to the selection of cheerleaders at high schools for U.S. military offspring. There was also the perception among African Americans that they would bear the brunt of cuts planned in the military in the wake of the erosion of the Cold War. Said Fletcher, "The feeling is that blacks are going to suffer more. The attitude is, 'They've used us up and we have no value anymore.'" Fletcher said he was struck by the desire of African Americans to speak out against racism. Some officers said they believe rating boards used for evaluation purposes are being used to "expel blacks" and they were told it would mean "the end of your career" if they took their complaint to equal opportunity offices.[14]

Affirmative action has been particularly effective in opening up fire and police departments to African Americans. Some would argue that these two agencies have been impacted most by the struggle for equity. For example, more than 20 years ago after mass struggle, court orders opened up a handful of Long Island, New York traditionally white fire departments to African Americans. But harassment and the like has reversed that small step. In Huntington Station, African Americans and Latinos make up 30% of the 89-year-old police department but are absent from the fire department. As so often happens when bias is perpetuated, "word-of-mouth" is the main mechanism for hiring and this invariably leads to the exclusion of minorities who are not plugged into these grapevines. This practice has been denounced repeatedly by the local NAACP and the Caribbean, Afro-American Olive Branch, a local advocacy group. The 17 April 1992 *New York Times* reports further that the fire department in the Big Apple remains the least integrated of all the city's agencies, with 423 Black firefighters out of a total of 11, 470. In part, discriminatory testing has been found to be a major culprit explaining this disparity, but unfortunately many white firefighters have been reluctant to accede to the demands of Mayor David Dinkins to alter such tests and open wider the doors of opportunity.[15]

Thus, despite decades of affirmative action, even agencies within the public sector that had been known for their progress toward equity have been regressing. Universities also had been known for being a bit more progressive on affirmative action questions. But that reputation, perhaps undeserved anyway, has also been shaken. The University of Maryland, for example, recently agreed to pay a total of $230,000 to as many as 267 Black job applicants who were allegedly passed over for secretarial and clerical positions because of their race. Mass struggle led to this settlement and the added affirmative action proviso—which amounts to a quota—that the university must extend jobs within the next three years to 60 African American applicants who were previously found to be qualified but who were not offered employment. These plaintiffs—who were in the overwhelming majority Black women—also demanded and won the proviso that supervisors should receive training in affirmative action and that job interviewing procedures would be standardized. This latter clause, as often happens in affirmative action struggles, will not just benefit African Americans but any who had not been part of the grapevine and the network that facilitated only certain individuals getting these jobs previously.[16]

African Americans have been able to win a number of affirmative action struggles. Yet, the prevailing tone set by the GOP nationally has encouraged an increase in employment discrimination and an undermining of affirmative action. Another case from Maryland—where mass struggle brought the perpetrators to justice—serves as a microcosmic example of what is happening nationwide. An employment agency in Rockville, Maryland has admitted that it turned away scores of Black applicants in the 1980s and has agreed to pay $50,000 to settle a lawsuit. Elliott Personnel Services sent away telephone callers assumed to be African American and racially coded its files, writing "short cropped hair" to denote Black male applicants and "straightened and restyled hair" to denote Black females. Over a ten-year period they engaged in over 1,000 discrete cases of such discrimination. According to the Equal Employment Opportunity commission, there has been an epidemic of such forms of discrimination by employment agencies. As of October 1991 more than 360 such complaints had been filed, a 20% rise over the preceding year.[17]

Affirmative action has been of urgent necessity when it comes to employment. The rising tide of racialism combined with the structural crisis of capitalism and the concomitant recession has provided a noxious brew for African Americans. Layoffs, firings, denials of jobs because of racism have been the inevitable result. Yet, as important as it may be, concentrating solely on affirmative action in employment, without examining the broader picture— e.g., housing patterns—would be mistaken. For as noted previously, as jobs flee to the suburbs, African Americans must follow, but racial barriers block the path.

Washington, DC—a predominantly Black city—is suggestive of what is happening nationally. For the third consecutive year the Fair Housing Council of Greater Washington reported in 1992 that discrimination against African Americans seeking to rent apartments increased. Black apartment seekers, they said, encountered discrimination 67% of the time. Bruce Kahn, a director of the council and Rabbi of Temple Shalom in Chevy Chase, Maryland reflected sadly that rental housing is "just one area of society" which has witnessed increased "bias and hatred."[18]

This housing discrimination also means Black families lose out in terms of wealth accumulation, for their neighborhoods often have been by-passed by the real estate inflation that has benefited so many white families. Housing discrimination also means that Black families have less options in terms of shopping for food, clothes and the like. The *Los Angeles Times* of 24 November 1991 concluded after an extensive examination that "residents in the predominantly black areas generally had to pay more for a poorer selection of goods. Residents of North Hollywood could frequently find better merchandise at lower prices, sold in air-conditioned stores...." What is even more curious is that median income in predominantly Black Inglewood is higher than predominantly non-Black North Hollywood, yet most major retailers stay away from the former and flock to the latter. This points up another fact relevant to affirmative action: there are those within the U.S. elite who recognize that affirmative action is necessary for the general health of the economy; but this perception competes with the idea that super-profits are to be made from discrimination and that discrimination is useful as a tool for dividing the working class.

Racism in Health Care

Because affirmative action has become a veritable lightning rod catching flak from various circles, some have suggested that these race-specific remedies be dropped in favor of "universal" programs, e.g., national health care. But recent studies suggest that discrimination lurks in this realm also, thereby making affirmative action still necessary here. For example, two recent reports have concluded that Blacks with kidney disease have to wait longer than white patients for transplants—if they get organ donors at all. Experts are not sure if the disparity is due to racism, economics, "genetics" or some combination of factors; others are not as circumspect, pointing to racism as the problem. In any event, Black patients wait 13.9 months for replacement kidneys while whites wait 7.6 months. This study was conducted by the federal Department of Health and Human Services. A separate study by the New York State Health Department found that a Black with kidney disease was only 55% as likely as a white to get a transplant. This disparity is even more appalling when it is considered that African Americans are more susceptible to kidney disease. Yet, according to the New York study, patients most likely to receive a transplant were male, white and residents of affluent neighborhoods.[19]

These studies illuminate larger factors. When a Black worker gets sick, he or she is less likely to receive prompt and adequate treatment, thereby harming chances to retain employment. Furthermore, affirmative action has to be viewed as an initiative that—if it is to be effective—must extend beyond the traditional areas of employment and education and extend to all areas of life. For if this expansion does not occur, racist toxins that exist in other areas of society will continue to erode whatever gains in employment and education take place. What is the gain if one secures employment via affirmative action and loses one's life because of racist health care!

For racism in health care does not just stop at organ donations and transplants. Black women over 40 have almost twice as many strokes as white or Latina women; strokes occur more frequently in Blacks of both sexes than in Latinos or whites. Dr. Ronnie Horner, co-author of the American Heart Association study that noted these facts, added that one reason for these disparities was limited access to health care. The National Center for Health Statistics recently concluded that life expectancy for African Americans was dropping precipitously, due to the explosion of AIDS, inadequate health care and other causes. Once again, affirmative action—or aggressive steps to alter the status quo—is necessary if equity and justice are to reign.[20]

Not surprisingly, African Americans and their allies have not been dormant in attending to the question of health care. Struggles have erupted nationally when efforts were made to close down hospitals in under-served communities; for example, Sydenham in Harlem or Homer G. Phillips in St. Louis. When these hospitals were shut down, it also meant the loss of jobs. Activists in New York City have sued a hospital over plans to move obstetrical care out of Harlem; groups in Washington, DC and several states have fought in court for higher Medicaid subsidies to hospitals. What NAACP Legal Defense Fund attorney Marianne Lado said about health care could be applied to other areas and underscores the continued need for affirmative action: "In principle, we eliminated segregation, but people still don't receive health care." This problem is exacerbated by the existence of "environmental racism," the fact that a disproportionate number of toxic waste dumps are sited in African-American communities. "What we have now is a two-tier medical system, at every step discouraging our use of it," according to Julia Scott, director of the Washington office of the National Black Women's Health Care Project. More pointed was a remark by Gordon Bonnyman, activist attorney from Tennessee: "Is there a role for the African American community to wield the power it did 30 years ago on the streets? Minorities will have to get out there and not play by the rules."[21]

Thus, affirmative action can be seen as the logical next stage of the civil rights movement. It is the effort to extend equity to all stages of U.S. life, it is a massive struggle for democracy. Failure to extend it in one area— health care—ineluctably has negative impact on other areas, e.g., employment. Yet, what is happening is that the GOP and their fat cat supporters have not been unsuccessful in hampering the advancement of affirmative action in employment and education, while blunting extension of it into such areas as health care and housing.

Racism in Higher Education

The area of higher education dramatizes with clarity the need for affirmative action. Post-secondary education is becoming more common. Production workers often receive skills upgrading at community colleges, for example. Yet, higher education is not free and federal aid has been essential. However, a recent study conducted by Prof. Alexander Astin of UCLA entitled *Black Undergraduate: Current Status and Trends in the Characteristics of Freshmen* presents troubling signs. Changes in federal financial aid policies during the past decade "have had a substantial impact on the black [student's] financial aid package. Fewer black [students] have access to federal grants and more must now rely on federal loans." This has led to a reduction the number of African Americans who attend college.

This is not a new trend but the culmination of long-term trends that reached a zenith during the Reagan-Bush Administrations. As a result, there has been an effort to provide special scholarship funds—a form of affirmative action—for African American students. Of late, this welcome trend has been under bitter assault by the White House and their acolytes. First of all, there was the demarche by the U.S. Department of Education to make such funding illegal. Mass outrage caused the Administration to retreat somewhat. Former Congressman William Gray, now head of the United Negro College Fund, compared the Administration effort to positions taken by David Duke: "It's beginning to smell awfully political to me. It has the stench of Louisiana politics."[22]

This stench was picked up by a three judge panel of the 4th Circuit Court of Appeals in Richmond, Virginia which declared that such scholarships offered by the University of Maryland are unconstitutional. Janell Byrd of the NAACP Legal Defense Fund was outraged, warning that the decision "could have a chilling effect" on affirmative action efforts by universities. This decision was even more ironic given the university's long history of Jim Crow. Now efforts to redress the lingering effects of that racism are deemed illegal. These racist initiatives have not been accepted with passivity. In March 1992 hundreds of African American students and their allies marched to the Capitol in protest sponsored by the U.S. Students Association.[23]

Racism in the Penal system

While blocked in their effort to obtain education, African Americans are being welcomed with open arms by the prisons. Ironically this is one of this society's most successful affirmative action programs or efforts at inclusion in that African Americans are over-represented as prison inmates. In California 1/3 of African American men in their 20s are behind bars, on parole or on probation. Their numbers—67,556—exceeds by nearly five times the number of African American men who attend four-year colleges in the state and is 10 percentage points higher than the number of young Black men nationwide who are in prison or otherwise under the control of the criminal justice system. By contrast the figure for white males is 5.4%, and 9.4% for Latinos. Lulann McGriff of the NAACP in San Francisco said the report had alarming implications: "We are writing off an entire generation of black men. Any time you have 33% under the thumb of the criminal justice system something is inherently wrong with the system."[24]

It is easy to infer that racial bias plays a role in producing such disturbing figures. A recent study by the U.S. Sentencing Commission shows that white defendants are more likely than Blacks to plea bargain their way out of tough mandatory prison sentences for drug crimes. A Connecticut study has revealed that there are severe racial inequities in the setting of bail. The *Hartford Courant,* in a computer assisted review of some 150,000

Connecticut criminal cases in 1989 and 1990, showed that "black and Hispanic men awaiting trial pay more than whites to get out of jail ... even when criminal backgrounds and kinds of crime are smaller." When drug charges were involved, the newspaper said, the disparities grew in bail averages by race.[25]

The fact about drug charges should come as no surprise. That the war on drugs has become a war on Blacks has long been common folk wisdom among African Americans. This has happened although the National Institute of Drug Abuse states that Blacks make up only 12% of the nation's drug users. In fact studies show lower percentages of African Americans using drugs when compared to white people in every age category. Nevertheless, the Center for Media and Public Affairs analyzed 800 news stories on the drug question from network newscasts and the *Washington Post*; out of more than 1,000 visuals depicting the human side of the drug problem—including pictures of crack houses and neighborhoods where drug sales or use were alleged to be prevalent—half the visuals showed only "non-whites", most of them African Americans. At ABC News, for example, 54% of the pictures showed only African Americans, compared with 29% that showed only Euro-Americans.

This practice is exacerbated by police authorities who use "profiles" to track down drug dealers. The problem is that to be a Black male automatically means you fit the profile, which means you will be stopped repeatedly and questioned. This "criminalizing" of Blacks, which could rightfully be called the ruling class' most effective affirmative action program in that it provides special attention to minorities, has been met with ferocious opposition from African Americans and their allies. Undoubtedly, the Minnesota Supreme Court felt the heat when it ruled in December 1991 that a state law is discriminatory against African Americans because it imposed stiffer penalties for possession of crack than for similar amounts of powdered cocaine. The former is cheaper and has flooded the streets of Black communities, while the latter is more expensive and more likely to be consumed in the suites. Of all people charged in Hennepin County in 1988 with possession of crack, 96.6% were Black; 79.6% of those charged with possession of powdered cocaine were white. The law in question called for a penalty of up to 20 years in prison for possession of three grams of crack, while possession of an equal amount of powdered cocaine carried a penalty of up to 5 years in prison.[26]

Access to Jobs is Basic

The thrust of civil rights forces has been to bar discrimination, but that is insufficient if African Americans are then left to languish in economic impoverishment. Even President Johnson recognized that civil equality by itself was insufficient in a 1965 speech: "You do not take a person who has been hobbled by chains and liberate him, bring him up to the starting line of a race and then say, 'You are free to compete with all the others,' and still justly believe you have been completely fair."

Civil rights forces and trade union forces were of like mind and thus forced Sears Roebuck in 1974 to adopt an affirmative action plan whereby each store was obligated to seek to reflect its area's population in its labor force of minorities and non-minority women. Failing meant the possibility of discipline for store managers. The obvious was discovered; i.e. the previously untapped pools of talent were now being tapped; affirmative action meant efficiency.

Unfortunately, all corporations did not move in this direction. Approximately twenty-five years ago there were 400,000 textile workers in Virginia, North Carolina and South Carolina but not one African American weaver, spinner or loom fixer. At Ford Motor plants in Atlanta, Memphis, and Dallas, African Americans were mainly used as janitors and toilet attendants. Yet this was not just a Southern question. In 1965 an NAACP investigation in Pittsburgh discovered a pattern all too typical of the building trades industry: No Black bridge and ironworkers. No Black carpenters. No Black electricians. No Black plumbers. No Black roofers. No Black tile-setters. So-called "white collar" work was also barred generally to African Americans. David Klein, a sales manager for the Wearever Aluminum Corporation based in New York City, testified before Congress that the company's rule was to discourage all Black job candidates.

This pattern of segregation also was operative at Duke Power Company in Draper, North Carolina. The plant's 81 white employees were technicians; Blacks were all janitors. These latter jobs were dirty and dangerous and unlike working as a janitor in an office building. In 1966 a number of African

American workers decided to protest this pattern and contacted the NAACP Legal Defense Fund. The company responded by claiming that if these workers sought to advance, they could take a test—though no such requirement had been placed on white workers. They decided to take the test for coal hauling—a job that mostly required brawn—and the test asked such questions as: "In printing an article of 24,000 words, a printer decides to use two sizes of type. Using the larger type, a printed page contains 900 words. Using the smaller type, a pages contains 1200 words. The article is allotted 21 full pages in a magazine. How many pages must be in smaller type?" None of the Blacks passed the test.

The Legal Defense Fund argued in court in the trailblazing case *Griggs v. Duke Power* that they were not against tests as such, but that these exams should have a correlation to the job performed. They argued that illegal bias should be measured not necessarily by motives—such thinking is often difficult to divine and prove—but by effects. In 1971 the U.S. Supreme Court agreed unanimously. The result was that African Americans were not limited to being janitors at Duke Power. The result was also that irrelevant tests that had served to bar not only African-Americans but many whites as well were called into question. The *Griggs* case was a major democratic victory for the entire working class and is emblematic of the struggle for affirmative action.[27]

Sad to say, victories like that achieved by progressive forces in the Minnesota Supreme Court case are at once limited and all too few. Similarly, ever since, the *Griggs* case has been subjected to severe erosion. The right wing has been able to convince all too many in this country that the reason for their deteriorating economic condition is not the rapaciousness of the ruling class but affirmative action. While Blacks are being scapegoated for the nation's ills, simultaneously racism is mutating and taking uglier forms. But African Americans are not the only group that is being battered by bigotry. Non-minority women, Native Americans, Latinos, Pacific Islanders and Asian Americans are only a partial list of those facing discrimination and in need of affirmative action.

3.

The Expansion of Affirmative Action

As noted, African-Americans have been in the vanguard of the struggle for affirmative action and they have been assisted by their allies, particularly some trade unions. And the constitutional basis for affirmative action remains—the 14th Amendment, which emerged after the Civil War—a conflict where the African American question was paramount. Moreover, in many regions of this nation the severe oppression inflicted upon African Americans makes affirmative action quite literally a matter of life and death. Yet, it would be false to see African Americans as the sole beneficiary of affirmative action or the sole recipient of discrimination. Strikingly, the right-wing tries to frame affirmative action as a "black question" alone, and thus play upon centuries of entrenched "Afro-phobic" sentiment to derail an initiative that has been of inestimable value for the working class in general and oppressed minorities and non-minority women specifically.

Women of all nationalities are both recipients of discrimination and its antidote, affirmative action. Unfortunately, statistics that are kept often do not disaggregate figures for minority women and non-minority women; however, it is clear that minority women are subjected to a particularly heinous "triple jeopardy," a textured, simultaneous, multi-layered discrimination based on gender, race, and class. Evn when disaggregation occurs, it is usually limited to "black-white" comparisons, thus leaving out what is happening to Latina, Native American and Asian/Pacific Islander American women.

For example, recent figures show that African American women in the past two decades have virtually closed the historical gap between their earnings and those of white women.

The median earnings of Black women working full-time and year-round is $17, 389 or 92% of the $18, 922 earned by similarly situated white women, according to the U.S. Census Bureau, citing 1989 figures. Women of all nationalities earn less than men, generally speaking. By contrast, Black men in 1989 earned 72% of the $28,541 earned by white men; twenty years ago the figure was 67%. Arguably, this gender gap is a function of gender bias that afflicts non-minority women and brings them closer to the level of minority women. This sea-change among Black women is largely a product of affirmative action, for in 1950s more than half of employed Black women were domestic workers, compared to about 3% today; undoubtedly, the struggle for affirmative action has been of great benefit to Black women because they had more ground to make up. Thus, we see the link between discrimination and affirmative action.

Still, the fact remains that African American women are more likely than Euro-American women to support a household on a single income, suggesting that even if earnings are similar, that of the former must be stretched farther. Moreover, despite the understandable focus on the Black male as an endangered species, the fact remains that Black women earn only 85% of the earnings of Black men.[1]

There are other unique issues, which suggest that just as there has been a special focus on the Black male, there needs to a similar focus on Black women. Black women are far more likely to suffer from breast cancer, diabetes, AIDS, hypertension, drug addiction, obesity, teenage pregnancies and emotional distress. Black women stand a one in 104 chance of being murdered, compared to one in 369 for white women. Lupus is three times more common among Black women. They are 50% more likely to become diabetic. They are more likely to suffer and die from cervical cancer. As many as 25% of Black female children are sexually abused by the age of 13. Evelyn White, an African-American woman author, in her recent book on Black women dealing with physical and emotional abuse has sought to link these troubling questions to the racist attack on Blacks generally, the misogynist attacks on women generally and the class warfare waged on the working class generally—Black women are being wounded simultaneously in all three battles. Black women have been forced to play a disproportionate role

as caretakers of the family and often this has led them to "defer
everything that has to do with them ... taking care of everyone
but ourselves." Of particular concern is her assertion that "50
percent of Black women live in a state of emotional despair."
This is at once a troubling commentary about what is happening to Black women and a severe indictment of a system that
has produced such a result.[2]

There are also special problems afflicting lesbian women, particularly lesbian women of color. These problems are particularly
noteworthy in the work place. However, Sandra Lowe, a "Black
Jewish" lesbian and an attorney for Lambda Legal and Education Fund, has stated that "women of color probably do not seek
legal help because it's a system that turns against people of
color"—thus linking the gender, ethnic and class dimensions of
the struggle.[3] When the civil rights community of California
united behind AB-101 which sought to bar anti-gay discrimination, it was vetoed by the GOP Governor, Pete Wilson.

Some economists have pointed to the horrendous discrimination inflicted on women generally as a major reason for the
lagging U.S. economy. Affirmative action is one of the surest
methods to aid in beating back the recession. The link between
discrimination and recession is as follows, according to these
economists: Women earn less than men and more of them entered the work force in the past two decades, thus adding millions of "cheap" workers. Simultaneously, unions were
bludgeoned and the minimum wage remained consistently
lower and less well-enforced than in Europe. As the service
industry, (disproportionately women) began to expand, U.S.
bosses hired this cheap labor and hedged on buying new equipment. This, it is argued, has meant lower output per worker. In
Germany and France, by contrast, where unions are stronger
and minimum wage laws more strictly enforced, there was
more investment in new technology. It could also be argued
that the low wages of many women workers has hampered
consumption and exacerbated the recession. As women become
an even larger sector of the labor force, this negative trend
could grow. Affirmative action, to insure that women were not
consigned to the lowest wage jobs—along with affirmative action to raise the wage levels of the lowest wage jobs—thus

becomes not only a question of equity but an anti-recession measure as well.[4]

Other economists have pointed to women as an under-utilized resource in the economy. Gender bias hinders women from realizing all of their talent, which ultimately is harmful not only to them but the nation as a whole. Clifford Adelman in his study for the U.S. Department of Education entitled, *Women at Thirtysomething,* concludes that "U.S. women of all races are the best educated and trained in the world." Women consistently have a superior academic performance—yet, this is not reflected in the work place. This academic performance has taken place in the face of formidable obstacles. A recent study by the American Association of University Women concluded that girls face discrimination from teachers, textbooks, tests and their male classmates. Teachers pay less attention to girls. Tests are biased against them. Textbooks ignore or stereotype women. There is a racial dimension too; when Black girls tried to approach teachers, teachers tended to rebuff them and paid more attention to white girls. Girls' self-esteem drops markedly, even more than that of boys, as they approach adolescence, and the sexist curriculum may be a contributing cause. Again, this discrimination is harmful to girls and the nation and affirmative action must be taken to insure that this pattern ceases.[5]

This kind of bias reinforces job segregation that forces women into low wage jobs. Women with four years of college earn roughly the same salary as men with only a high school diploma and the gap worsens as women get older. By the time she is between the ages of 55 and 64, the average female worker is making $.54 for every dollar earned by a man. Equal pay for equal work is the law but that is not the issue here. The issue is job segregation—or comparable worth, as it is often called—which means that "female jobs" pay less, e.g., clerical, nursing, social work, public school teaching, etc. To its credit, unions like the American Federation of State, County and Municipal Employees, have waged determined struggles to erase this sexist gap. For example, in April 1991 AFSCME reached a $7.5 million agreement to raise wages of 911 dispatchers—predominantly minority women—who were paid less than mostly male fire department dispatchers. Yet, wage inequity persists

in part because sexism—like racism—is profitable to the few
though it harms the many. Affirmative action is needed, both to
raise the wage levels of low-paying jobs held by women and
integrate women into other jobs traditionally barred to them. In
the latter category, the United Mine Workers has been helpful
in bringing women into coal mining jobs.[6]

The comparable worth struggle waged by many unions has
been a major preoccupation of affirmative action advocates.
Twenty-two states and the District of Columbia have studied
the issue and six —New York, Washington, Oregon, Wisconsin,
Iowa and Minnesota—altered their pay structures. States spent
an estimated $500 million on wage adjustments as a result.
The province of Ontario in Canada has gone further. Since 1988
both government and private-sector employers there have been
required to study their labor force for gender-based wage discrimination and make appropriate adjustments. In the U.S.,
comparable worth struggles generally have been limited to the
public sector, a frontier that has to be crossed in the 1990s is the
further extension of this concept in the private sector.[7]

There are other issues involving women workers of all nationalities that cannot be ignored. As reported in the 25 March
1992 *Washington Post*, the "future issues" team of the General
Accounting Office—the investigative arm of Congress—recently
concluded a major study on employment trends involving
women workers. In 1960 only 18.6% of married women with
children under 6 were in the labor force; today it is closer to
60%. Moreover, their percentage in the government sector is
growing more rapidly than in the private sector. Given the
growing percentage of women in the labor force generally, the
GAO counselled that on-site or near-site child care facilities be
established, that flexible work schedules and leave policies be
implemented, etc. The GAO study has been bolstered by a recent study by Professors Ann Wendt and William Slonaker of
Wright State University in Ohio. They studied 2,000 employment discrimination lawsuits filed between 1985 and 1989 and
found that nearly a quarter of the women who took maternity
leave had no job waiting for them when they wanted to return
to work. By contrast, only 2% of women taking leaves for other
medical conditions lost their jobs. Another recent study by
Laurence Levin and Joyce Jacobsen found that women who

interrupt careers for family never make as much money as female peers who stay on the job; generally, if a woman took six months off over a 20-year period, she would be doomed to earn less than women who did not take such leaves. Such policies are not only misogynist, they are anti-family and anti-child—despite the inflated rhetoric of the GOP Right which purports to be the ultimate defender of the family. Affirmative steps must be taken to override this obnoxious discrimination. Yet, the response to these trailblazing studies has been minimal from the bosses thus far.

Sexual harassment in the workplace should be viewed in this context. In addition to being a raw expression of power and misogyny, it is also a tool to subordinate women, keep them in their place and prevent them from joining the struggle for wage equity and affirmative action. This underscores the importance of a recent Ninth Circuit Court of Appeals decision that defining what is sexual harassment should be viewed not from the perspective of the reasonable man—of course—nor the reasonable person, but the reasonable woman. This trailblazing decision outraged Bush appointee U.S. Attorney William McGivern, who inferentially linked the commonality of struggles of minorities and non-minority women. He warned that this would lead to a situation where *cases involving racial discrimination would have to be judged from the perspective of the reasonable African American.* Precisely! Forcing bosses and courts to view bias through the unique lens of the victims of this poison is a giant step on the path to effective affirmative action.[8]

This decision is even more important when one ponders the meaning of a Roper Organization poll. Over 3,000 women were surveyed and it was found that as more women enter the labor force, the more likely they are to develop a dislike for men. Sexual harassment, especially from bosses, is one cause. They found that 20 years ago 70% of women believed "most men are basically kind, gentle and thoughtful." But by 1990, 40% of women felt "most men are basically selfish and self-centered." An inevitable aspect of Cold War induced ideological underdevelopment combined with gender bias is the proliferation of what some have termed the "war of the sexes." Affirmative action serves to empower more women and thereby serves to strike a blow for equity.[9]

Again, gender bias in the workplace has a racist edge. In May 1990 Cheryl Smith, a light-skinned African American woman, had been serving four months as a para-professional at PS 33 in the Bronx. But when she revealed in casual conversation that she was Black, she was fired by her white female supervisor and replaced by a white woman. Such actions also hamper relations between women across racial and ethnic lines. Stricter anti-bias laws are needed, not least to curb such conflicts.[10]

For it is clear that one of the tactics of affirmative action opponents is to foment squabbles, particularly between oppressed minorities and non-minority women. Such dust-ups have occurred frequently in the context of struggles over set-aside contracts for businesses. The Congressional Black Caucus has addressed this conflict as it was manifested in the debate over the multi-billion dollar Surface Transportation Act. The U.S. Department of Transportation had administered two separate programs, for women-owned enterprises (WBE) and minority business enterprise, (MBE), until 1987, when the two were combined due to a cutback in federal funding. Since 1987 contracts for women have risen steadily from 2.7% in 1985 to 5% in 1990, while the minority proportion has slipped precipitously from 12.7% in 1985 to 9.3% in 1990. Combining the two meant the original 3.2% women-owned business goal mandate was "collapsed" into the 10 percent goal mandated for all minority owned business, including minority women. Congressman Edolphus Towns of the CBC added, "An unintended consequence has been to foster competition and conflict between two disadvantaged groups which the disadvantaged business enterprise programs were designed to benefit." Combining the two meant "forcing two disadvantaged business groups to compete against one another, (and) has undermined the original legislative intent to expand their overall participation in surface transportation procurements." Recently Congresswoman Eleanor Holmes Norton—who is Black—introduced an amendment to seek to solve this conflict but the monopoly sector of the construction industry blocked her welcome initiative. No doubt affirmative action opponents have an interest in disrupting accord between natural allies.[11]

These are not easy questions. Kathleen Blee in her book, *Women of the Klan*, reminded us that the KKK was not an all male fraternity. Writers like Alice Walker and Ntozkae Shange have reminded us that sexism is not imbedded exclusively in white males. The ideological underdevelopment of the U.S., a partial product of the Cold War and Red Scare, does not help. Moreover, male supremacy, which predates capitalism—unlike white supremacy which grows out of capitalism—in a sense can be seen as especially difficult to eradicate even in a transition to socialism. Even advanced detachments of the movement have had difficulty in grappling with such real and apparent contradictions. African National Congress lawyer Albie Sachs, in calling for affirmative action in South Africa, noted the phenomenon of men who were freedom fighters by day and (in the home) fascists by night. At the ANC Congress in the summer of 1991 there was sizeable and spirited opposition to imposing a 30% quota of women on the National Executive Committee, the leading body. Certainly there are differences between ethnic and gender struggles. For example, the struggle for African American equality tends to be a multi-class struggle, while there are those who would dispute characterizing women's struggle for equality similarly; in some ways, it does appear easier to integrate women—especially white women like Katharine Graham, Nancy Kassenbaum, Jacqueline Onassis, Carla Hills, Christie Hefner, Jeane Kirkpatrick, et. al.—into ruling circles. In any case, combining questions of ethnicity and gender are complex and it is understandable why a Black woman in Congress like Norton would take the lead in resolution.[12]

But such initiatives and strengthened affirmative action will not come easy. The reasons why are adumbrated in Susan Faludi's book, *Backlash: The Undeclared War Against American Women*. She argues forcefully that the bourgeois media and the right-wing particularly have distorted and mis-characterized reality in a manner disadvantageous to women. They have sought to blame the increasing stress of women—emotional, economic and otherwise—not on misogyny but on feminism. They have sought to portray day care not, as a useful tool for families generally and working women particularly, but as a tool disintegrating the family.

This is bad enough but bias does not end there. Just as we speak of institutionalized racism, which affirmative action is designed to redress, we must also speak of institutionalized sexism. It is inured in the marrow of society. Just as African Americans face health care barriers that lead to negative repercussions in the work place, the same can be said for women of all nationalities. Much of the medical research in the U.S. sponsored by the National Institute for Health and other institutions exclude women. According to Congresswoman Patricia Schroeder, this means "American women have been put at risk." Hence, doctors cannot be sure exactly how drugs tested on men will behave in women. Trials of new AIDS therapies are heavily biased toward men even though this plague is increasingly impacting women. Similarly research into psychological disorders is biased, says Dr. Susan Blumenthal, chief of the National Institute of Mental Health. Women are believed to metabolize certain antidepressants differently than men. Even the rats used in many of these studies are male! Questions such as breast cancer, contraception, and postpartum depression are not adequately studied. Of the more than 2,000 researchers at the National Institute of Health, only three are specialists in obstetrics and gynecology.[13]

Thus, to pursue affirmative action in the workplace alone is insufficient if women are being handicapped in other areas of society. Ultimately to be effective affirmative action—a core component of the battle for democracy—must be extended broadly to all areas of society.

Like African Americans, women of all nationalities often face bias from the same body they seek to redress their grievances: the U.S. Congress. On the whole, women are paid 78% as much as male Senate aides largely because they are over-represented at the lower rungs and barely represented at the top. This study, which was conducted by the International Brotherhood of Teamsters, the Communications Workers of America and the National Rural Letter Carriers' Association, presents a disturbing picture of sexism at the highest level of government.[14]

Another study by the Center for Women in Government at the State University of New York at Albany arrived at similar conclusions, adding the point that minority women have fared even worse than white women. But with all of its problems, the public sector has been more responsive than the private sector in addressing discrimination, precisely because it is more democratic. Affirmative action has been pursued more vigorously in government; after all, at least 50% of the electorate are women. The Los Angeles City Council and the LA County Board of Supervisors have recommended formally that gender balance be followed in appointment to boards and commissions. Yet, what makes government look good is the horrible record of the private sector, not their realization of equity.[15]

This terrible record is especially apparent when considering affirmative action in areas traditionally barred to women, e.g., the police force. This is particularly troubling since studies indicate that women are less likely to use excessive force when on duty. According to Katherine Spillar of the Fund for the Feminist Majority, "Both the research in the United States and internationally shows that women police officers are less authoritarian and use force less often than their male counterparts. They are better at defusing potentially violent confrontations, possess better communications skills, and respond more effectively to incidents of violence against women." These words were confirmed by the Christopher commission that investigated the L.A. Police Department in the wake of the beating of Black motorist Rodney King. There were no female officers among the 120 officers with the most "use of force" reports despite the fact that female officers comprise 13% of the force. Not one woman was listed among the top 132 officers in another ranking of officers by use of force, personnel complaints and officer-involved shootings. Women officers appear to be less personally challenged by defiant suspects and feel less need to deal with defiance by immediately using force or confrontational language.[16]

Despite these obvious assets, women in the LAPD—as in other departments—have faced a veritable reign of terror. Often they are shunned, isolated, harassed and discriminated against. According to Police Chief Darryl Gates, they face even more harassment than gay males. The mostly male LAPD also exhibits profoundly sexist attitudes toward women in general, particularly in cases of domestic violence. But the LAPD is not alone. Deanna Hall is a police officer in the Detroit suburb of Novi. Though eight months pregnant in December 1991, she was not allowed a leave and could not afford to go on unpaid leave, and thus was working a grueling 7 a.m. to 7 p.m. shift. Plus she was suffering verbal harassment from her bosses. During her third month of pregnancy she strained a stomach muscle while subduing a drunken prisoner but the two days of disability leave she took triggered a wave of verbal abuse. Her union has been unable—or unwilling—to win better terms for pregnancy in collective bargaining with management. Federal anti-discrimination law requires employers to treat pregnancy as they do other temporary nonduty disabilities. In 1976 Chief Justice Rehnquist wrote an opinion for the high court declaring that the General Electric Company did not violate federal sex discrimination laws when it excluded pregnant women from its otherwise all-encompassing disability coverage. The company treated men and women equally, said the Chief. Yes, said the dissenters, if men got pregnant, they would not be covered either! In response Congress passed the Pregnancy Discrimination Act of 1978 requiring that employers treat pregnant women "the same" as men and insisting that women be evaluated only on their "ability or inability to work." That same year, the California legislature said employers must allow pregnant women up to four months of unpaid leave to recover from childbirth and guarantee that they would get their jobs back after maternity. When California employers challenged this law in the Supreme Court in 1987, Rehnquist sided with them, showing no deference to the legislature. Fortunately, he was on the losing side, though this case ultimately was of little help to Deanna Hall.[17]

The LAPD and the case of Deanna Hall are symptomatic of what is happening to gender-based affirmative action. Diversity brings enrichment to the labor force, as the special skills of female police officers suggests. Diversity also is a benefit to the working class as well, who are less subject to being brutalized when officers are female—a factor that is not negligible given the historic role police have played in beating strikers, breaking strikes, squashing peace rallies, etc. Like other aspects of the struggle for democracy, affirmative action brings a more humane society closer to reality.

The U.S. military rivals police departments in resistance to gender-based affirmative action. Retired Navy Commander Kay

Krohne recently conducted the first in-depth study of the problem of sexual harassment in the Navy. The conclusions were both predictable and stunning. Sexual harassment lowers the productivity of women and ultimately of the Navy by forcing women to spend time and energy fending off unwanted advances. Of those she interviewed, a whopping 65.5% said they had been harassed. Her findings dovetail with a 1990 Defense Department report that found 64% of women in the U.S. military had been sexually harassed. She argues that the Navy does not take sexism as seriously as it takes racial harassment and racism. As in other forms of bigotry, the perpetrators engage in massive denial, arguing that no real problem exists. It is bracing to contemplate that if those subjected to military discipline engage in such male supremacist conduct, what is taking place in the civilian sector where no such discipline exists?[18]

Actually, the military is only following the lead of its corporate sponsors. Though studies show that failure to utilize the talent of women is harmful to the economy and not particularly efficient for the corporate sector, hostility to gender based affirmative action exists in practice—despite their honey coated words in support to the contrary. A study by the Feminist Majority Foundation found that less than 3% of the top jobs at Fortune 500 companies were held by women in 1990; only 175, or 2.6% of the 6,502 corporate officers employed at the nation's largest companies in 1990 were women. The FMF blamed the disparities on sex discrimination and an "old boy" network. Eleanor Smeal, former president of the National Organization for Women who now heads the FMF commented,, "At the current rate of increase in executive women, it will take until the year 2466—or over 450 years—to reach equality with executive men."[19]

The FMF study served to confirm a study done earlier by the U.S. Labor Department which pointed to the existence of a "glass ceiling" blocking women's advancement. They pledged a nationwide crackdown on those who violate anti-discrimination and affirmative action laws, though personnel to conduct such probes is quite limited. Hence, only a major push from women's groups and their allies in the trade union movement can insure a reversal of this troubling pattern. For akin to stereotyping of

African Americans, a 1990 survey by Catalyst, a New York based research firm, found that nearly half of the human resource managers thought that women had less initiative than men and were less willing to take risks. women are also perceived as being less committed to the job. However, this stereotype is dead wrong, as confirmed by a 1990 report by Wick & Co., a Delaware-based consulting firm, indicating that frustration with career progress—grounded in sexism—led most women to leave jobs. Some companies have engaged in affirmative action to overcome these sexist hurdles, e.g., holding seminars seeking to educate male managers, making the promotion of male managers contingent on how diversified their staff is, etc.[20]

Like the inclusion of more women police officers, the inclusion of more women in the corporate sector helps to bring a change in the culture. At least that is the result of a study done by Judy B. Rosener of the University of California-Irvine. She found that successful women tend to motivate their co-workers and staff by sharing information and power—in contrast to their male counterparts who relied more on the traditional organization structure of carrots and sticks. Increasingly, this traditional style is being criticized and a number of commentators have contrasted this style with what is perceived as a different style practiced in Japan—allegedly more akin to feminine practice here at home. The Rosener study must be approached cautiously for as Carol Tavris points out in her important book, *The Mismeasure of Woman*, practices of women often are valorized on the premise that they stem from some inherent form of feminism, when in fact they stem from a context that consigns women disproportionately to powerlessness. In any case, resistance to affirmative action for women can be seen in part as a resistance to anti-authoritarianism, a resistance to a humane approach.[21]

Studies and more studies are being conducted but the reality remains: gender bias and resistance to affirmative action designed to remedy it. Roberta Spalter-Roth, director of research at the Institute for Women's Policy Research in Washington has a response. She calls for enforcement of pay-equity laws and stepped up unionization. "The laws are on the books and should be enforced," she says.[22] But many of these laws are federal and dependent upon enforcement by a GOP that has been actively hostile to questions of equity. Unionization is needed but there is the double whammy of a right-wing dominated National Labor Relations Board that sees blocking unionization as a major mission, and the AFL-CIO led by Lane Kirkland, which seems most energetic about destabilizing socialist regimes and less enthusiastic about responding to class warfare at home. Nevertheless, the example of AFSCME in bringing pay equity and comparable worth to thousands of its members shows what is possible.

Women of all nationalities not only face grueling discrimination and hostility to affirmative action in the corporate suites, the shop floor, the police department and the military. They face a similar fate within the professions. Again, this sexism is a waste of "human capital," not to mention a continuing violation of the law. A study conducted by the American Medical Women's Association and the Feminist Majority Foundation found that not a single dean of a U.S. medical school is a woman, that 98% of department chairs are men and that medical school faculties are still 79% men, despite the fact that 36% of all medical students are women. Comparable worth struggles are needed desperately here, in that 84% of physicians are men and 97% of nurses are women, with the latter being subjected to lower wages and more onerous working conditions. Even doctors trained to deal with women have not escaped the maw of bias. The American College of Obstetricians and Gynecologists has never had more than two women in its top 17 offices at any one time in its 41 year history. The American Medical Association, the largest organization of doctors in the world, has never had a woman as chief executive officer in its 144-year history.

Medicine is a hybrid profession featuring doctors in private practice and doctors in the working class employed by huge hospitals. Indeed, the long-term trend seems to be of the latter growing and the former shrinking. As such, consider this: women who are doctors made only 62.8 cents per dollar of their male counterparts in 1988. Experience is not the factor explaining this discrepancy. The average net income of men with one to four years' experience in 1987 was $110,000, while women with the same experience made $74,000, on average. This suggests that raw sexism is at play here.[23]

Affirmative action of all sorts for women is a dire necessity in the field of medicine. This means increasing their numbers in medical school and their rate of employment in hospitals. Most of all, a change in the culture is needed. It is not unknown for women to be barred from certain classes in medical school, e.g., urology, sexually transmitted diseases, etc. This is like fighting medical ailments with one arm tied behind one's back. In a national survey of third-year medical students published in the Journal of the American Medical Association in January 1990, 87% of the women students said they had been subjected to sexist slurs. More than half reported having been the object of sexual advances, and nearly one third felt they had been denied opportunities in their training because they were women. Medical school professors tend to pay more attention to male than female students. This blatant misogyny is not only harmful to women; it is harmful to this nation in that it hampers the full development of half of the brain power of this nation so necessary to combat illness and disease.[24]

Trends akin to medicine can be found in law. Here too there is a trend for women attorneys to be employed in the public sector, or as workers more than as private practitioners. Here too women are generally unrepresented at the highest levels. Here too there is a culture of sexism that serves as a formidable barrier against affirmative action. In a survey of women lawyers conducted by the *National Law Journal* it was found that 60% of the respondents said they experienced sexual harassment. Three-quarters of the respondents feel that they do not have the same opportunities as men to cultivate social activities so important for obtaining promotions and job assignments. More than half of the respondents say that their male superiors are less willing or not willing at all to serve as mentors for women lawyers. Sadly, this sexism also extends to law school where similar practices and attitudes are readily found.[25]

Academia is no safe harbor for women either. Female faculty and staff members are paid less than men with jobs of equivalent rank, are more likely to hold lower-level positions, and receive fewer job promotions. Women who are oppressed minority, older, disabled, or lesbian face "double" or even "triple" discrimination, according to these studies. Unsurprisingly, African American women carry a special burden. A report released in the fall of 1990 by the University of Kentucky found that a white man has a one-in-four chance of being employed in the highest job rankings, while a white woman's chance is one in ten. The likelihood of an African American woman being employed in the highest ranks is approximately 1 in 33.[26]

When the University of Kentucky was confronted with this outrageous reality, it took affirmative action. Over $2.5 million was provided to a fund that was used for pay adjustments and pension contributions to female employees. Yet even this notable move fell far short of what was needed; addressing sexism in the workplace via affirmative action was neglected. This has been the unfortunate trend in the U.S.: gathering dust on shelves is study after study documenting a heinous bias, while scant attention is paid to the kind of affirmative action remedies that could right these wrongs.

To its credit the U.S. Congress did seek to take affirmative action in addressing the fact that broadcast licenses are held disproportionately by men. Congress held that the Federal Communications Commission could take gender—among other factors—into account when awarding these plums. When Clarence Thomas was on the federal court, this case came before him. There was evidence to suggest that he had issued his opinion by the time he came before the Senate Judiciary Committee for confirmation to the U.S. Supreme Court, though this reality was kept shrouded by the evasive nominee. After he was safely confirmed, the opinion was released and in a staggering blow against gender based affirmative action, this mild remedy was ruled illegal by Judge Thomas.

This blow against affirmative action was deemed even more remarkable in that in June 1990 the U.S. Supreme Court ruled that similar affirmative action for oppressed minorities was constitutional. More remarkable was that Thomas—who has painted himself as a non-activist judge, deferential to elected bodies—rejected Congress's finding that employing gender as a factor was critical to accomplishing important governmental objectives. This Thomas opinion will be used as precedent to invalidate other forms of gender-based affirmative action.[27]

As if these setbacks were not bad enough, a recent study by the New York City Department of Consumer Affairs—reported in the 13 March 1992 *Wall Street Journal*—notes that divorce lawyers often shortchange women clients. This follows other studies which indicate that women tend to suffer grievously after divorce, certainly more so than men. Sadly, the surge to power of the Reagan-Bush Administration has eroded further the already perilous position of women of all nationalities.

Affirmative action for oppressed minorities and non-minority women tends to be linked. The mostly African American led civil rights movement benefited non-minority women, for example. Yet, while keeping this thought firmly in mind, it is important to recognize that all of these questions of bias have a special character. Take the issue of affirmative action for Latinos. This is a heterogeneous community that groups under one rubric a number of distinct ethnic groups including Chicano/Mexican-Americans, Puerto Ricans, Dominicans, Cuban-Americans, Central Americans, South Americans, et al. Studies that focus on "Latinos" or "Hispanics" might lead one to assume that there is little difference between, say, Cuban-Americans and Puerto Ricans; in fact, there are crucial differences. Moreover, many Mexican-Americans are indigenous and could in another context be considered Native Americans.

Still, keeping those important caveats at hand, it is well to note that there are disturbing trends buffeting Latinos that only aggressive affirmative action can remedy. Often these problems are overlooked, in part because a significant percentage of this community is first generation immigrant and have not been able to build the kinds of organizations that are so familiar among African Americans and non-minority women. Furthermore, there are great stretches of this country without significant Latino populations, which makes pressuring Congress more problematic. In addition, Clete Daniel in his *Chicano Workers and the Politics of Fairness: The FEPC in the Southwest, 1941-45* suggests that focusing on the problems of African American workers does not necessarily lead to the total addressing of the special problems of Latino workers.

This backdrop helps to place some of the recent studies focusing on Latinos in proper perspective. The Census Bureau reports that Puerto Ricans continue to be this country's poorest community. Of the 2.5 million Puerto Ricans living on the U.S. mainland in 1990, 41% of the individuals and 38% of the families were impoverished. That compares with a total U.S. poverty rate of 14% for individuals and 11% for families. Other Latino groups also fared better than Puerto Ricans, including Chicano-Mexicanos (individuals 28% and families 25%), Cubans (17%-14%), Central and South Americans (25%-22%), and other Latinos (22%-19%). Affirmative action in the workplace is needed desperately because lack of jobs is a major explanation for these disastrous figures. Puerto Ricans have the lowest rate of participation in the labor force of the groups reported (53% for men and 42% for women), compared with a non-Latino labor force participation rate of 74% for men and 57% for women.[28]

These kinds of figures are no freak of nature but stem directly from a distinct bias directed against Latinos. Consider the aforementioned study, *Opportunities Denied, Opportunities Diminished: Racial Discrimination in Hiring* that focused primarily on job bias aimed at African Americans. The Urban Institute, which published this study, conducted an earlier study in Chicago and San Diego in 1989 focused on Latinos and non-Latino whites. They discovered that in general African Americans appear less likely than Latinos to be denied equal opportunity for advancement through the hiring process but more likely than Latinos to be denied a job that is offered to a comparable non-Latino white applicant. Latinos were much more likely to experience unfavorable treatment at the application and interview stages than were African Americans. At the application stage, the incidence of unfavorable treatment of Hispanics was 6% (compared to 2% for African-Americans), and at the interview stage, the incidence of unfavorable treatment of Latinos was 18% (compared to 7% for African Americans).

The authors suggest that employers could identify Latino applicants by their accents during the initial telephone contact. Therefore, Latinos could be denied the opportunity to apply even before visiting the employer in person. Black and non-Latino whites could be less easily identified by voice. It is possible that documentation requirements under the Immigration Reform and Control Act may help to explain the bias directed against Latinos.

That this study was not inaccurate is suggested by a recent study conducted by the Fair Employment Council of Greater Washington and reported in the 29 April 1992 *Washington Post*. A woman identifying herself as Juanita Alverez called an optometrist's office in suburban Virginia to apply for a receptionist's job advertised locally. She was placed on hold for five minutes, called by the name "Carmen" and told that no more applications were being taken. Thirteen minutes later another woman with the same qualifications called to apply for the job—she did not have a Hispanic surname or accent—and was given an appointment for an interview.

Studies also show that the typical male Latino applicant is more than twice as likely to encounter discrimination as the typical Latina. Strikingly, discrimination occurred just as often among companies that advertised as "Equal Employment Opportunity" companies. Like African Americans, Latinos face residential segregation that exacerbates this kind of employment discrimination. Indeed, according to a study conducted by a consulting firm hired by the federal government and reported in the 18 March 1992 *Washington Post*, Latinos were more likely to live in segregated neighborhoods at the end of the decade of the 1980s than at the beginning.

Whatever the case, it is clear that Latinos face special forms of discrimination in such discrete areas as accents, language, and immigration law that require a special approach. Affirmative action becomes the mechanism to overcome this institutionalized pattern of bias.

Few could deny that affirmative action is a pressing necessity. Speaking of Latinos, Sonia Perez of the National Council of La Raza, has averred, "They're in the labor force. They're working. But if you look at the type of jobs, you'll see they are concentrated in low-wage jobs." How true. The right-wing assault against trade unions and the general de-industrialization of the economy has had a special impact on Latinos. Nearly 30% of all Latino men are working in assembly-line jobs or as laborers in industries like construction, while just 19% of men in the non-Latino population are working in those job categories. Another 17% of Latinos are in the service industry; for non-Latinos the figure was 10%.[29]

There is some evidence to suggest that the bosses are seeking to take advantage of Latino workers by consigning them to the dirtiest and most dangerous jobs. Indeed, Latino factory and industrial workers have a higher rate of injury on the job than non-Latino white and Black workers in similar jobs. Many of these workers are immigrants; however, studies in California, Illinois and New Jersey show that Latino workers—both documented and undocumented—have injury and illness rates on the job three times higher than non-Latino whites who take the same jobs. Black workers suffer higher rates than whites too, but lower rates than Latino workers. Discrimination on the basis of national origin is a major reason for this carnage; many Latino workers are operating complex machinery and handling chemicals, but directions are often in English. Many of the immigrants fear deportation and are not necessarily inclined to object. Joseph Kinney, head of the National Safe Workplace Institute has put it bluntly, "What we have here is a fairly vicious economic situation where employers are chasing lower costs, which leads them to Hispanic workers. Part of the dictum of lower costs is to squeeze the people of wages, benefits and safety. Their expectations are so low, so abuse is invited."

And the abuse is of such a magnitude to be mind-boggling. The New Jersey Department of Health found that the finger amputation rate for Latino workers was 52.8% for 100,000 as against 28.9% for 100,000 for Blacks and 9.5% for 100,000 for non-Latino whites, and that the fatality rate for Latino construction workers was 34.8% for 100,000 workers as against 24% for Blacks and 10.6% for non-Latino whites.

The California Department of Health has found that 49% of the workers with the highest level of lead in their blood were Latino—a rate nearly twice that of their ratio in the state's population. The Los Angeles County District Attorney's office has prosecuted 45 employers for grievous workplace health and safety violations over a 6-year period, with almost all of the cases involving Latino workers.[30]

As with African Americans, affirmative action for Latinos is a question of life and death. Unless urgent measures are taken to upgrade the jobs to which Latinos are consigned—providing adequate Spanish language instruction for complex machinery, for example—and upgrading occupational safety and health laws, along with other forms of affirmative action, the plight of Latino workers will continue to worsen. This will continue to drag down the standard of living for the entire U.S. working class.

This situation is even more of emergency proportions because demagogic politicians are beginning to focus on Latino immigrant workers as the reason why working people generally in this nation are suffering. Obviously this is a massive falsehood but when broadcast repeatedly over the airwaves and printed in the press, this charge takes on a certain air of authenticity. What needs to be broadcast is that immigrants and their offspring contribute mightily to the economy by paying billions in taxes, by working tirelessly in jobs, by revitalizing deteriorating neighborhoods. For example, in Los Angeles County undocumented workers mostly from Mexico generated almost $3 billion in assorted tax revenues during 1990-91. This study by the *Los Angeles Times* of 6 January 1992 found that most of these taxes are flowing to Washington—$1.7 billion—in the form of income and Social Security taxes. But Washington's GOP-inspired effort to slash revenue sharing with state and municipal governments has increased the burden of L.A. and has fueled immigrant bashing.

Clarity is crucial on such an issue but it seems that this is precisely what is lacking. The state population of California actually grew at a faster rate from 1950-70 than 1970-90; but the looting of state and municipal treasuries by GOP-elected officials and fat cats has meant that education and social services have suffered. And immigrants are being pointed to as the scapegoats.[31]

It is important to keep in mind that ethnic bias is not a static phenomenon. Bias against the Irish was rife in the 19th century but has diminished since then. It very well may be that the militant fightback of African Americans has caused the bosses to heighten bias against Latino workers on the premise that a significant percentage are immigrants and less likely to complain for fear of deportation. Whatever the case, it is apparent that affirmative action to redress the bias directed against Latinos is needed desperately.

Like African Americans and non-minority women, Latinos face bias not only in the private sector but the public as well. In California, which has the largest Latino population in the nation, the state Senate Office of Research has noted that although they comprise 25% of the state's population, they held only 11.3% of 2.5 million "white collar" jobs; yet they held 37.8% of nearly 1 million "blue collar" jobs and 33.6% of service jobs. African Americans, on the other hand, accounted for 7% of the state population and 7.3% of "white collar" jobs; Asian-Americans also exceeded parity, comprising 9% of the population and 11.2% of these jobs. This study suggests that in California affirmative action in both the private and public sector—to upgrade certain jobs and insure that Latinos are represented with parity in others—is mandatory.[32]

The scapegoating and bias aimed at Latinos is imposing a crushing burden on the youth. The number of Latino children living in poverty in the U.S. grew by nearly a third during the past decade, a rate that easily outpaced similarly escalating rates among African American and non-Latino white youth. The rate for Latino youth was a 29.3% increase; though they account for only one-ninth of the total child population, they accounted for almost half of the total growth since 1979 in the number of children living in poverty. Again, this is not just an immigrant phenomenon, because Puerto Rican youth—who are citizens—account for a sizeable percentage of the increase.[33]

Like African Americans and non-minority women, Latinos also suffer from severe medical problems due in part to bias, that if unchecked, can wipe out affirmative action gains in other fields. Latinos have poorer access to medical care than others in this country, principally because they work in lower-paying jobs without the benefit of medical coverage. The General Accounting Office has stated that 33% of Latinos had neither private nor public medical insurance, a rate which they said is larger than African Americans and non-Latino whites.[34]

This kind of bias in health care is replicated in education. According to a report filed by the National School Board Association, "Hispanics are now significantly more segregated than blacks.... Hispanics in California in 1988 were in schools with fewer non-Hispanic whites than were black students in Alabama or Mississippi...." But like African American students, Latinos are concentrated in poor school districts that spend less per pupil than most.[35]

As a partial result of this pattern, in 1990 only 54.9% of Latinos graduated from high school, about the same proportion as 10 years ago; this is more than 20 points below the proportion of Black students who graduated and nearly 30 percentage points below that of non-Latino whites. College attendance rates are lacking as well, along with college faculty employment; only 2.1% of tenured faculty at UC-Berkeley are Latino and only 2.7% of administrators are Latino. Affirmative action has been pursued to correct this pattern; this has included more emphasis on bilingual education, special scholarship programs, more Latino faculty, etc. But the right wing has been working furiously to undermine such laudable initiatives.[36]

Because of these atrocious patterns of bias, affirmative action has become a major demand of Latinos and their allies. A major victory was won recently in L.A. County where it was decided—after mass pressure—that if a third of applicants for jobs in, e.g., the county's huge public hospital system are Latino, then a third of the hires must be Latino. This was in response to an accusation by the Equal Employment Opportunity Commission in 1990 that the county was discriminating against Latinos. What is striking about this proposal is not only the fact that a number of Latino organizations objected, feeling that the proposal did not go far enough; it is also striking that what is involved here is a de facto quota. Again, though quotas are routinely reviled by demagogic politicians, they are just as routinely imposed because quotas are one of the more direct affirmative action mechanisms to overcome institutionalized bias.[37]

California is not only the home of the nation's largest Latino population, it also has the distinction of having the largest Asian American population as well. Like the Latino population, this is a heterogeneous grouping. There are Japanese American and Chinese American populations whose roots in this country reach back to the 19th century. There are Korean American and Cambodian American populations whose vintage is more recent. Asian American also refers to the sizeable population whose roots are in India. Theoretically, the term Asian American refers to any population in this country whose ancestry is based in Asia; this could include those of Thai, Vietnamese, Laotian, Burmese, Taiwanese, etc. ancestry; it could include the large Iranian, Pakistani and Afghan-derived populations. Yet, when this population is considered, usually referred to is the Japanese-American, Chinese-American and Korean-American populations. The Pacific Islander population is often grouped with the Asian-American population. This nation's long and imperialist relationship with the Philippines perforce suggests that bias and affirmative action are key concerns with this grouping. Yet, the Pacific Islander population also includes Aleuts, ethnic Hawaiians, Polynesians, etc.

Akin to Latinos, Asian Americans vary widely between and among the various ethnic components. In cities like Long Beach and Lowell, Cambodian Americans are living in desperate straits. In cities like Monterey Park, California and the suburbs outside of Vancouver, BC extending into Washington, there are Hong Kong Chinese populations that are quite affluent. Yet, irrespective of income level it is accurate to suggest that Asian Americans face a common bias based on national origin, appearance, and the like.

This is especially true given the rise of Asian economies including Japan, Korea and Taiwan, which has led to a spate of "Japan bashing" that has had no small impact here at home. The situation has become so severe that the U.S. Civil Rights Commission issued a recent report charging that anti-Nippon hysteria has generated ethnic animosity toward Asian-Americans. The case of Vincent Chin—the Chinese-American murdered by unemployed Euro-American autoworkers outraged by the success of Japanese imported cars—is evidentiary of what is going on. Federal statistics on hate crimes against ethnic and religious minorities have been collected only for a year or so. Still, the fragmentary reports are shocking. Although Asian-Americans were only 4% of Philadelphia's population, in 1988 they were victims of 20% of the city's hate crimes, making them statistically more likely to be victimized that African Americans, Latinos, or the Jewish population. Throughout the 1980s in Los Angeles, 15% of hate crime victims were Asian Americans, who constituted 8% of the city's population.[38]

Asian Americans not only face hate crimes, they frequently are denied equal access to a decent education and the voting booth and often are treated unfairly by the police and the courts. Akin to other ethnic minorities, others often are of the opinion that Asian Americans face no such harassment and, in fact, are favored. This is far from the truth. Take the question of accents, a point of discrimination that afflicts all ethnic minorities to a greater or lesser extent—even African Americans who have been in this nation for hundreds of years. Rambhai Patel, whose roots are in India, was dismissed from his post as credit manager of Eiki International because it was suggested that his accent was not good for the company's image. This kind of discrimination is heavily racist and Euro-centric for it is well recognized that it is considered chic for a worker to speak with a British or French accent. Cases like that involving Rambhai are becoming all too common.[39]

The internment of Japanese Americans during World War II is emblematic of the depth of anti-Asian bias in this country. The eclipse of the Soviet Union has led to a heightening of inter-imperialist contradictions, particularly between the U.S. and Japan. This increasingly strained relationship is leading to a mutation of racism in the U.S., accompanied by a profound racial anxiety being felt by U.S. elites. Andy Rooney, the $800,000 per year CBS commentator, who was suspended from his post because of anti-Black and anti-gay remarks, did not attract any attention when he mockingly referred to Rockefeller Center as "Lockefella Center" (after a purchase by Japanese interests) and added, "I'm vaguely anti-Japanese. Don't ask me why. Just prejudice, I guess. I'm very comfortable with some of my prejudices and have no thought of changing them now."[40]

Lee Iacocca, whose salary has topped $18 million yearly in a government subsidized corporation, symbolizes much that is wrong with monopoly capital, has been in the forefront of Japan-bashing. He led the charge during President Bush's ill-fated trip to Tokyo in January 1992. Monopoly capital often is pointed to as the source for racism and clear evidence for this proposition emerges when the epidemic of anti-Asian sentiment is examined.

Apparently this is not enough for U.S. elites; they also are seeking to turn other oppressed minorities against Asian Americans and vice versa. Conservative GOP Congressman Dana Rohrbacher of California sought to create a firestorm by charging that Asian Americans were being denied admission to the University of California because allegedly unqualified Afri-

can Americans and Latinos were being admitted. This demarche was condemned by Joseph Watson, Vice-Chancellor at
U.C.-San Diego. He charged that the Congressman was using
this issue to attack affirmative action in higher education: "To try
to generate racial conflict is dastardly, particularly by a Congressman."[41]

The fact is that a number of so-called elite schools have de
facto negative quotas that place an artificial ceiling on admission of Asian Americans; mathematics scores on standardized
tests, in which many Asian Americans make high scores, are
devalued in admissions decisions and English language profi-
ciency is valorized. These schools tilt the playing field in favor of
the sons and daughters of alumni, who are overwhelmingly Euro-
American. Not surprisingly, the old canard of "merit" rarely en-
ters into these discourses.

The government has been quite slow to address this discrimination. According to the *Chronicle of Higher Education* of 1
April 1992, more than a year and a half after the Education
Department found that the University of California, Los Angeles discriminated against some Asian American applicants, the
department has taken no action against the institution. The
private sector has been engaging in similar forms of discrimination. Despite her success at the Winter Olympics, Asian American gold medalist Kristi Yamaguchi has not received the
number of offers from Madison Avenue and major corporations
as previous winners have. It is suspected widely that anti-
Asian bias is the cause.

Asian Americans and Pacific Islanders often are viewed as
recent arrivals on the U.S. scene and this is brought forward as
a basis for the discrimination they face; the assumption being
that bias will dissolve with time. Of course, their arrival is not
altogether recent but, in any case, the example of Native
Americans—the first Americans—suggests that date of arrival
is irrelevant when it comes to racism. Their percentage of the
population in states like South Dakota and Montana makes
them the most sizeable ethnic minority. Native Americans also
comprise a sizeable percentage of the population in states like
Oklahoma, New Mexico and Arizona, just as the people who are
referred to as "Eskimos" are a sizeable percentage in Alaska.

Like Latinos and Asian Americans, the rubric Native Americans refers to diverse peoples, e.g., the Lakota of the Dakotas, the Hopi and Navajo of the Southwest, the Cherokee of Georgia, the Iroquois and Mohawk of New York, the Chumash of California, et al. Yet, whether one is referring to the East Coast or West Coast, the South or the North, the numbing statistics remain the same. Native Americans remain at the bottom of the ladder when it comes to employment, infant mortality rates, life expectancy, rates of higher education and the like. Native Americans also face special insult—the naming of professional athletic teams in Washington, DC, Cleveland and Atlanta after Indians, which holds an entire people up for ridicule. Native Americans are consigned to reservations, a policy not unlike the failed "bantustan" policy of apartheid South Africa. Their unique religious rites often are circumscribed by the government. Treaties negotiated between sovereign Native American states and the U.S. government have been honored more in the breach than the observance. Political prisoners like Leonard Peltier are living symbols of what happens to Native Americans when they seek to protest against these constant outrages.

The *Washington Post* of 25 March 1992 reports on the dire circumstances faced by Native American youth. By the end of high school, because of the bleakness of their future, 1 of 5 girls and 1 of 8 boys have attempted suicide. In 1986 the rate of death for Native American youth was 190 deaths per 100,000 population, compared to 81 per 100,000 among all U.S. teenagers. Genocide against this population is not just a subject of historical vintage; it is an ongoing reality. Affirmative steps must be taken to reverse this age-old pattern of bigotry.

Affirmative action as a policy was broached initially as a policy designed to address bias directed at African Americans. But gradually it was seen that affirmative action should be extended to others. Increased misogyny, increased immigration and Japan-bashing has caused bias to mutate and take on new forms. This suggests that affirmative action should be expanded and thereby the struggle to expand democracy should be expanded. This is especially critical in the workplace but affirmative action also must reach the sphere of access to capital as well.

4.

Access to Capital:

Croson and the New Legal Basis for Affirmative Action

In addition to employment and education, affirmative action has been pursued in terms of access to capital. There has been a decided struggle to insure that businesses are owned by racial and ethnic minorities and non-minority women and to insure that banks and insurance companies are not allowed to discriminate. Minority owned businesses particularly tend to employ ethnic minorities, thus assuaging the Depression era levels of unemployment that have afflicted these communities. This too is part of the struggle for democracy, and like other forms of affirmative action has the added component that aid to these small businesses is objectively a blow to monopoly capital. For example, to this point there has been affirmative action pursued by the Federal Communications Commission to insure that minorities and non-minority women receive broadcast licenses. Now that policy is being revised and it is apparent that the major beneficiary will be monopolies like NBC and CBS, which will now be able to snap up more radio stations. Minority-owned stations like WLIB-AM in New York City have been in the forefront of political struggles like the anti-apartheid movement and the effort to elect the first African American mayor. One can expect reasonably that no such struggles will be led by radio stations owned by NBC or CBS.

At times it seems that howls of outrage are uttered more fervently when affirmative action is applied to business enterprise. It is almost as if some U.S. elites are willing to bite the bullet and for the sake of efficient deployment of human capital are willing to accept affirmative action in employment and education; however, when it comes to potential business competitors, a wall of opposition arises. This is even more unusual when one considers how state monopoly capitalism has provided consistent and constant aid to businesses over the years: "cost plus" or no loss contracts to Pentagon contractors, subsidies to agri-business, subsidies to exporters—the list is veritably endless. At moments of rare candor, elite spokesmen concede that affirmative action has been practiced between and among elites for some time. Former chief U.S. trade negotiator Clyde Prestowitz confessed in *The Economist* of 30 November 1991 that after deregulation, the U.S.'s AT&T and Japan's Nippon T&T had "huge structural and historical advantages ... To level the playing field, both countries applied special restrictions to the operations of the giants while, in effect, helping newcomers with affirmative action." The beneficiaries were such giants as GTE, MCI, U.S. West, NYNEX, Pacific Telesis, etc. Unlike affirmative action for minorities and non-minority women, this did not become a controversial issue.

This kind of affirmative action has not allowed minorities and non-minority women to challenge monopoly frontally; at best, it has been of benefit in the realm of small business.

But even here, the old elite reigns supreme. According to the U.S. Census Bureau, small businesses owned by Euro-American males had far greater revenues than those owned by racial and ethnic minorities and non-minority women during the 1980s. The former tend to be concentrated in manufacturing or wholesale, while the latter tend to flock to services, where receipts are not as high. Firms owned by men of Asian-Pacific Islander origin averaged $189,000 in receipts; firms owned by Latino men averaged receipts of $66,000; African American men, $50,000; Native American and Alaska native men, $47,000. Firms owned by women, regardless of nationality, had receipts far below those of men of a similar nationality. For example, white males' small businesses on average had receipts of $189,000 and that of white women, $70,000; for African American women the figure is $41,000. Strikingly, minority-owned firms are heavily concentrated in just four states: California, Texas, New York and Florida.[1]

What is happening to African American entrepreneurs is symptomatic—in a general sense—of what is happening to minorities and non-minority women generally. African Americans make up more than 12% of the nation's population and only about 3% of its businesses—and those businesses account for just 1% of all sales. A major problem is insufficient financing, a problem that can be laid at the doorstep of banks. A study published in the Spring 1988 issue of the *Review of Black Political Economy* found that white, Latino and Asian American owners of established businesses enjoyed a 90% success rate in obtaining loans from commercial banks, while African Americans with identical business credentials were successful only 66% of the time. The combined total assets of all 36 of the nation's Black-owned banks are only $2.1 billion—less than the $2.4 billion in combined total assets of the two biggest Latino-owned banks in Miami. This latter factor further reduces the ability of minority business to succeed.[2]

A disheartening new study, "Black America 1991: A Special Report of Business, Economics and Politics," published by the National Association of Black Journalists, rings the changes. In assessing the decline of Black business they point to the anti-affirmative action policy of the Reagan-Bush Administrations, particularly the reneging of the federal government on promised contracts. The Department of Defense, they say, has "not once in five years met a congressionally mandated goal of awarding five percent of its contracts" to minority firms. Those minorities seeking to do business with the government must fill out a "voluminous and invasive" 70-page certification document that labels the applicant as socially and economically disadvantaged. NABJ also complains about the expansion of the definition of minority business, which now includes, they say, Hasidic Jews and other white men.

Despite the obstacles, Black businesses have been around since the 1600s. In those days, there were African Americans who ran inns, barbershops, ice houses and even ship builders. In Pittsburgh Ben Andrews provided meat to the Revolutionary War soldiers at Fort Duquesne. Yet, what happened to Tunsford Lane in 1830 is suggestive of what has happened to Black business and why affirmative action is necessary. He operated a successful merchandise store in Raleigh, North Carolina—until angry whites drove him out of business and out of town. A similar process took place after the Civil War, this time aimed

at Black skilled workers and craftsmen. The question is: what
is the remedy for this wrong? Are we supposed to dismiss this
outrage as a trivial chapter in history, best forgotten? Or, in the
best traditions of U.S. law, should we take steps to make the
victims whole via affirmative action?[3]

The bias may not be as blatant but it continues nonetheless.
Pacific Gas & Electric in California, the super-rich monopoly, is
well on it way to reaching a 20% goal for purchases from
women-owned enterprises and has made progress in awarding
contracts to Asian American controlled firms; however, African
American firms continue to be overlooked. One aspect of affirmative action that cannot be ignored is that monopoly capital may
be less prone to accord affirmative action to African Americans
than others.[4]

This should not be interpreted to mean that non-Blacks are
doing well in this field. The largest government agencies in
California are doing a poor job of opening up the bidding process to underrepresented groups, according to a new report from
the state auditor general. The report examined $3.7 billion in
contracts from the five state agencies that do the most procurements. It showed that minorities captured only 4.5% and non-
minority women only 2.4% of the contract work. The agencies
studied were the California State University system and General Services, Department of Corrections, of Transportation,
and Water Resources. The latter three agencies have done virtually nothing to implement the law and the others had done
next to nothing.[5]

As the National Association of Black Journalists' report suggested, one of the worst transgressors has been the Pentagon.
In 1990 the Pentagon awarded $123.8 billion in contracts; of
those, $24 billion, or 19.3% was awarded to small business. Yet
the number of so-called "small and disadvantaged businesses,"
which includes ethnic minority and non-minority women businesses, that received contracts was a paltry 2.9%. Henry Wil-
fong, president of the National Association of Disadvantaged
Business, has scoffed at the Pentagon notion that such set-
aside programs jeopardize national security! The Pentagon
"gives us all kinds of reasons why it hasn't complied with the
law. They say they can't find us. When we find them, they
wonder if we're qualified. When we're qualified, they lament

the fact that we didn't get in at the start of the job. They sincerely promise to include us, 'next time,' or in 'the next proposal.'" Fed up, Congresswoman Cardiss Collins has introduced new legislation to correct this wrong, though the right-wing has pledged to block it.[6]

There are other policies and legislative initiatives that are being pursued that are worthy of emulation. In Atlanta Mayor Maynard Jackson has implemented new Equal Business Opportunity legislation to mitigate the effects of bias. The program offers bonding, financial and technical aid to these businesses. The program was passed unanimously in September 1991 despite opposition in monopoly circles. The Atlanta initiative inspired Mayor David Dinkins of New York City to move along similar lines.[7]

The Oklahoma Department of Commerce has initiated "Black Gold," a one-year pilot program that began in August 1991, which makes financing and tax incentives available to Black-owned businesses that relocate or establish new firms in Oklahoma. The program also has made attempts to expand many of the 3,461 existing Black-owned firms in the state. Instead of providing incentives to encourage monopolies to locate within their borders, states would be well advised to target such incentives at minority and non-minority women-owned businesses.[8]

Though California State University has lagged in affirmative action in contracting, the University of California has sought to embark on a different path. This has been due in large part to mass pressure. But U.C. has not been typical of the academy. More typical is Rutgers University, which has implemented a $510 million five-year building project, which includes the construction of a new $1.2 million Paul Robeson Cultural Center. E. Harvey Meyers, the architect for the Robeson center was, as of August 1991, the only Black entrepreneur involved in the project. And his contract was worth only $60,000.[9]

When one examines the direct policies of monopoly capital, it is easy to trace the source of invidious bias to their doorstep.

This is particularly true for finance capital, banking and insurance. California Insurance Commissioner John Garamendi has held hearings that indicate that African Americans are forced to lie about their residences in order to obtain auto

insurance. A Black Oakland businesswoman, Selwyn White-
head, told Garamendi of her attempt to buy commercial insurance in 1987; companies knowing she was calling from a
minority-owned business quoted her prices of $8,000 to
$10,000. But when she pretended she was the secretary to a
white man, the price came down to $1,200.[10]

Insurance companies and banks have been similar in their
patterns of discrimination. Steven Roth, president of Barry
Leeds & Associates, a New York market research firm for
banks, is in a position to know about this. He sent one white
and one minority "shopper" to 50 bank branches in middle-class
neighborhoods that were predominantly white. He found that
the minority shopper waited significantly longer for service and
received explanations of mortgage products that were far less
comprehensive. He added, "Each had the right profile to obtain
a mortgage, but the bankers seemed to have two different
standards for responding." He found "a subtle pattern of discrimination that started almost as soon as a black walked in."
Such patterns are indicative of the toxic impact of racism;
banks in this country by and large have a weak bottom line and
one would expect they would be clamoring for business—yet
they're turning away customers on grounds of race and/or ethnicity.[11]

The Roth study and the studies cited below are evidentiary
of why firm numbers, even quotas, are needed. The miasma of
bias is so pervasive that only firm numbers can insure that it
can be overcome; anything else can degenerate easily into mere
window-dressing and lip service.

In New York City, for example, the largest banks have been
engaging in a pattern of redlining and discriminatory home
lending practices, according to a study released by ACORN (Association of Community organizations for Reform Now).
ACORN concluded that the bias in lending is not based just on
income but was more a function of race, since banks were more
likely to reject high-income applicants whose properties were in
neighborhoods where most residents were minorities than they
were in those that were predominantly white.[12]

For those who feel ACORN's study was infected by some sort
of left-wing bias, this notion was vitiated by a study that came
to similar conclusions, authored by the Federal Reserve. They

found that even poor whites get mortgages more easily than affluent minorities. Their study reviewed 6.4 million loan-application records from 9,281 lending institutions. It revealed that in 1990, 33.9% of Black applicants and 14.4% of white applicants were turned down for mortgages; 26.3% of Blacks and 12.1% of whites were denied government-backed mortgages. This is putatively violative of the Community Reinvestment Act. Congressman Kwesi Mfume has introduced legislation that would strengthen the Equal Credit Opportunity Act to allow for punitive damages against CRA violators. Again, this admirable proposal has been opposed stridently by high level banking circles.[13]

Bank of America, one of the largest U.S. banks, has been a particularly odious violator. Under pressure they have been forced to adopt affirmative action in this area by offering easier terms to those applying for loans in low-income areas, providing incentives to loan officers to make low-income loans and providing special appeals procedures for those whose applications are denied. Yet, none of these items tackle head-on the race-specific forms of bias that transcend class. However, their effort to hire more minority loan officers may be helpful in that regard.

This banking bias is even more extraordinary for it amounts to Black bank depositors subsidizing non-Black areas. In Los Angeles, Bank of America and Security Pacific Bank together held $631 million in deposits in predominantly Black South Central L.A., but lent only a combined total of $11 million to area customers for home mortgages. Like a colonial outpost, these millions from South Central flowed out to Beverly Hills and similar areas. This pattern is not just peculiar to Los Angeles. Manufacturers Hanover had over $100 million in deposits from Harlem but made only $100,000 in annual mortgage loans there.[15]

What is happening to African American farmers is indicative of what is happening to many minority entrepreneurs. According to the 14 March 1992 *New York Amsterdam News*, 34,000 Black farmers lost their land in the 1980s. African American farmers lose 500,000 acres of land annually. They are losing land at a rate 10 times faster than their Euro-American counterparts. There have been affirmative steps to build co-ops and there have been efforts to force Congress to pass the Minority Farmers Rights Act; yet the steady erosion of land ownership by Black farmers continues.

Thus one sees that minorities and non-minority women are denied access to capital for businesses, for homes, etc. This pattern of bias caused many agencies, municipalities, etc. to enact legislation to "set-aside" a percentage of contracts for businesses controlled by those who traditionally have faced bias. This affirmative action was part of a democratizing process, but in 1989 the U.S. Supreme Court in *Croson v. Richmond* ruled that such affirmative action was unconstitutional.

As a result, set-aside legislation has been wounded. At least two dozen cities from coast to coast have suspended their set-aside programs voluntarily or under court orders. So have many states, including New York, New Jersey and California. Similar programs are being challenged in court or are under review in most of the 32 states, in 200 cities and countless counties and public authorities that have them. Fortunately, the ruling in *Croson*, did not directly impact federal programs but politically the impact overall has been devastating—particularly in the midst of a recession. After *Croson* a third of the members of the United Minority Enterprise Associates, a trade association for Black building contractors, went out of business. Some of the "minority" and "women" owned businesses that have survived have been fronts for enterprises actually controlled by white males.[16]

The City Council of Richmond, Virginia—cradle of the Confederacy—passed the Minority Business Utilization Plan at issue in *Croson* on 11 April 1983. The Plan obligated primary contractors that were allotted construction contracts to subcontract at minimum 30% to minority business enterprises (MBE); the plan was scheduled to last for 5 years. An MBE was defined as a business at least 51% of which was owned and controlled by "citizens of the United States who are Blacks, Spanish-speaking, Orientals, Indians, Eskimos or Aleuts." This affirmative action could be waived if it was deemed impossible to find MBEs. The Council had found that though Richmond was half African-American, only .067% of the city's construction contracts had been awarded to MBEs during the 1978-83 period. A former mayor had testified that "without equivocation" the local construction industry "is one in which race discrimination and exclusion on the basis of race is widespread." The Council also relied on the fact that nationally there was discrimination in the industry, a reality that impelled Congress in 1977 to pass a similar law which was upheld by the high court in 1980 in *Fullilove v. Klutznick.*

J. A. Croson Co., a non-minority firm, bid on a city construction contract and sought a waiver of the affirmative action provision, averring that no MBEs could be found for subcontracting. Their request was denied. Croson then sued the city, claiming that the MBE violated the 14th Amendment of the U.S. constitution, mandating equal protection under the law.

This was the sixth case in which the U.S. Supreme Court addressed the constitutionality of the "use of race-based measures to ameliorate the effects of past discrimination on the opportunities enjoyed by members of minority groups in our society," i.e., affirmative action. In these cases, starting with *Bakke* and up to *Croson,* the high court has ruled that affirmative action is not unconstitutional as such. However, in *Croson,* the court restricted severely the constitutionality of affirmative action.

They distinguished *Fullilove,* and suggested that Congress has more latitude than state and local governments to impose affirmative action. Yet, they argued in a 6-3 decision that non-congressional bodies face more restriction; worse, their decision was premised on the Constitution itself—not interpretation of a statute—which gives this horrible decision more reach and impact. However, *Croson* does not apply to gender-based affirmative action, which raises the old suspicion that U.S. elites are more willing to accommodate white women than oppressed racial and ethnic minorities. Unless this decision is reversed, *Croson* could sound the death knell for affirmative action, just as it has been used to this point to gut affirmative action for MBEs.

What was particularly galling about the reasoning in *Croson* was that for the first time a court majority ruled that benign racial classifications enacted by local government in order to remedy the impact of bias against minorities are subject to "strict scrutiny," the same draconian criterion of constitutional adjudication accorded "invidious" racial classifications that discriminate. When this criterion is used—e.g., a law that says whites can vote but Blacks cannot—the classification inevitably fails. *This suggests that measures to impose racism should be viewed through the same lens as measures to eradicate racism!* This also reinforces the notion that the court is more concerned with the "plight of white males" allegedly harmed by "reverse discrimination" than the continuing corrosive impact of racism.

Also shocking was Justice Antonin Scalia's suggestion that the court was particularly suspicious of affirmative action in this case because the "dominant political group" in the Council, which was also the "dominant racial group," was the moving force. This kind of thinking, reminiscent of the most hysterical nightmares of white racist South Africans, is shocking. Scalia has evinced no such concern about majority white bodies enacting laws impacting minorities. Moreover, the court majority looked askance at the very notion that bigotry may have played a role in explaining why minorities received so few contracts— and this in a land suffused with Jim Crow and its residue!

Croson is a chamber of horrors and a mightily suggestive hint as to how the high court—now featuring Clarence Thomas—will judge affirmative action plans underchallenge by racists in the future. If nothing else, this opinion is a clarion call to minorities, non-minority women and their trade union allies to rally to preserve and expand affirmative action; for reliance on this court is foolhardy, and only the court of public opinion should be addressed with confidence of receiving justice.

5.

The Civil Rights & Women's Equity Act of 1991

It has been well known for some time that racism and anti-communism are two of the major weapons for the U.S. ruling class's ability to retain power. Now with the apparent easing in relations with Moscow, what some have called the "erosion" of the Cold War (combined with heightened destabilization of former Soviet power), it seems there has been a similar contradictory trajectory of racism.

The veto of the Civil Rights Act of 1990 by President George Bush (before he was forced to sign its 1991 equivalent) was sobering news to those who have pointed to the U.S. as a citadel of human rights and democratic practice. It came in the wake of an escalation of racist violence, the Persian/Arabian Gulf crisis (which heightened discriminatory impulses) and an economic tailspin.

The post-election speech of Jesse Jackson at Spelman College in Atlanta in the fall of 1990 summed it up. The future, he argued passionately, is imperiled by what he called "the shaking white hand theory—a weak, scrawny, shaking white hand" that has a job taken away by "a strong black hand."

This picture derives from a television ad showing white hands crumpling a job rejection letter because a workplace "quota" dictated that the job must go to a minority. The ad was placed by close Bush ally Sen. Jesse Helms and his re-election campaign; it is credited by some as mobilizing certain white voters, thus guaranteeing a victory over the then surging challenger, African-American Democrat Harvey Gantt.

This same image was played on by "former" Nazi and Ku Klux Klan leader David Duke in his surprisingly strong showing in the race for the U.S. Senate is Louisiana and his equally strong run for Governor in 1991. "Blacks as scapegoats," was Jesse's summary of this trend.

This is nothing new. The Reagan-Bush team used the misogynist and racist image of the "welfare queen" to triumph in 1980. Kicking off an electoral campaign in Philadelphia, Mississippi—where the martyred civil rights workers were murdered in 1964—was their trademark. In 1988 Bush used the image of Willie Horton in an attempt to intimidate certain white voters (some pundits are suggesting that an ad campaign focusing on Saddam Hussein as Willie Horton rather than as Hitler be considered). "Playing the race card" has been a staple of U.S. politics for at least 200 years.

Bush and his clique felt even more constrained to take this tack in light of the impact on the Democrats of Kevin Phillips and his *The Politics of Rich and Poor*. In the midst of the economic slowdown in Japan manifesting in the summer of 1989 (in the middle of the often tense Structural Impediment Initiative talks and the resultant reluctance by Tokyo to continue financing the U.S. government), Bush felt compelled to go from "no new taxes" to "mo' new taxes." Naturally he wanted to give his close buddies in the elite a capital gains tax *cut* and force the rest of us to pay more. Phillips had reassured the Democrats that it was okay to begin discussing the class question—after a significant hiatus—and their leaders in Congress began discussing "soaking the rich" during the budget negotiations (of course they were at best sprinkled in the end). And just as in Bacon's Rebellion in the 1660s, Bush sought to play the "race card" and seek to convince white workers that they had more in common with their brethren in the elite than their brethren across color lines in their class. The Civil Rights Act of 1990 was vetoed on the spurious ground that it was a "quota" bill in a complimentary complement with Helms' TV ad. Inevitably this was viewed negatively, particularly by the disproportionate number of Black and Latino troops in the sands of the Saudi sexist empire. The President has yet to recognize that it is difficult to ride two horses going in different directions at the same time.

But if it were only Bush and his clique—even within the government—that would be one thing, but increasingly we have had to contend with a U.S. Supreme Court and imitative lower court judges who often are to the right of Bush-Reagan on legal questions in the old "good cop-bad cop" routine. It should not be deemed surprising that the successful fight to keep Robert Bork off the high court was one of the major victories of progressive forces in recent years. In part this is because many in the civil rights lobby have since the onset of the Cold War* stressed court action over mass action.

Unfortunately, we were not able to keep off the court Antonin Scalia, Anthony Kennedy, David Souter, Sandra Day O'Connor and Clarence Thomas; and we were not able to prevent William Rehnquist's promotion to Chief Justice. This is not to mention blocking the path of the scads of district court and courts of appeal judges who shape and mold the law.

This has had particularly devastating impact on affirmative action. The Civil Rights Act of 1991 was introduced in part to overturn the toxic impact of five 1989 decisions by the high court that sought to turn back the clock. A spirited mobilization of pro-affirmative action forces, the backlash against the White House's Clarence Thomas nomination and the revulsion against the David Duke race combined to force Bush to sign this legislation; yet, despite this Herculean effort we are still burdened by another 1989 court decision that unlike the five was grounded in the constitution and not statutes; thus, according to the civil rights forces, this cannot be overturned by a statute like the Civil Rights Act of 1991.

This ticking time-bomb based on the U.S. Constitution is *City of Richmond v. J. A. Croson Co.* In a patently dishonest decision the high court struck down a minority business set-aside program (e.g.,allocating a certain percentage of contracts). In 15 of the 55 cases involving challenges to set-asides so far since *Croson*, jurisdictions have successfully defended programs from being declared unconstitutional by courts or from being halted by temporary or permanent injunctions, according to the Minority Business Enterprise Legal Defense and Education Fund (MBELDF) in Washington, DC. However, lower courts have judged nine programs unconstitutional, including

---

* Cf. my *Black and Red: W.E.B. Du Bois and the Afro-American Response to the Cold War, 1944-63* (Albany: SUNY Press, 1985); *Communist Front? The Civil Rights Congress, 1946-56* (London: Associated University Presses, 1987); *Black Liberation/Red Scare: Ben Davis and the Communist Party* (Newark: University of Delaware Press, 1993)

the City of Atlanta, the Florida Department of Transportation, the State of Michigan, and the Philadelphia School Board. And 20 state and local jurisdictions have voluntarily suspended their programs or ended them. In the midst of economic recession this has injured the minority business sector and their disproportionately minority workforces.

So, the civil rights forces decided to go after the "easiest" goal first and get Congress to overturn the high court's novel reading of the Civil Rights Act of 1964 and Section 1981 of the Civil Rights Act of 1866 in those five decisions. Three days after Bush's veto and nine days before Congress adjourned for the year of 1990, the Senate failed by one vote to override the veto, thus delaying until the 102nd Congress the attempt to reverse (the) discrimination of the Supreme Court.

Though the Civil Rights Act of 1991 speaks to race, gender, national origin, color, religion, etc. and thereby benefits the overwhelming majority of peoples of this nation, Bush and his party—who are looked to by some, believe it or not, as the avatars of human rights—have persisted in portraying it as a bill for Blacks only and have persisted in throwing sand in the eyes of the masses.

Their failed attempt to appoint the failed drug czar, William Bennett (who is addicted to tobacco), as chief of the Republican Party replacing the then ill Lee Atwater, was further evidence of the White House trying to play the race card. In his opening press conference, Bennett sought to talk about nothing but "quotas." The late Mr. Atwater had promised jobs for minorities in party posts and within the administration and held out the hope that some might be elected to the GOP national committee (of elected members from the 50 states, one was Black then, and none is Black now; about 20% of the elected members of the Democratic National Committee are Black). Fortunately a blatant conflict of interest that even the GOP could not swallow forced Bennett to stand down and refuse the post. But once again, Bush and Co. were trying to ride off in different directions at the same time. They want to make quotas the question of the moment, though the Civil Rights Act of 1991 explicitly stated that it was not a quota bill (although this was probably an acceptable compromise, goals, timetables, and, yes, quotas, should not be ruled out of bounds in principle).

Thus, with this backdrop, it can be seen easily that the Civil Rights Act of 1991 and its still controversial aftermath has been and will be an occasion for a titanic struggle that will help to define the trajectory of the 1990s as we go into the next century. We know that the existence of Jim Crow presented an aching contradiction for Washington seeking to win "hearts and minds" in a Cold War world; Jim Crow had to be eroded; but if the Cold War has eroded, a different scenario may present itself to civil rights forces.

Thus, understanding with some specificity elements of what the Civil Rights Act of 1991 entails and what helped to propel it is needed now more than ever.

Brenda Patterson sued McClean Credit Union where she had been working under Section 1981 of the Civil Rights Act of 1866. Her claim was that her employer had harassed her on the job, failed to promote her, and then discharged her, due to racial discrimination. She presented substantial evidence to back her claim but ultimately the high court ruled bizarrely that Section 1981 applies only to discrimination in "the formation of a contract ... not to problems that may arise later from the conditions of continuing employment...; (the) right to make contracts" on an equal basis with white citizens the court ruled "does not extend ... to conduct by the employer after the contract relation has been established, including breach of the terms of the contract or imposition of discriminatory working conditions." Hence, Patterson could prevail in her discrimination claim only if she could establish that the promotion "involved the opportunity to enter into a new contract with the employer." But this is absurd; when one seeks promotion at many jobs, negotiating a new contract is not at issue nor contemplated. Effectively this meant that in the midst of this recession when many workers cannot readily leave one job for another, Brenda Patterson had to suffer abuse. For unlike Title VII of the Civil Rights Act of 1964, which applies only to employers with 15 or more workers, section 1981 covers work sites of all sizes; she had to sue under 1981 and thus like 11 million other workers similarly situated, according to the fine and detailed report put out by Senator Kennedy and his staff of the Committee on Labor and Human Resources, Patterson, et al, "lack *any* (emphasis-EMK) protection against racial harassment and other forms of race discrimination on the job."

According to Julius Chambers, Director-Counsel of the NAACP Legal Defense and Education Fund, Inc., since *Patterson v. McLean Credit Union*, more than 200 claims of race discrimination have been dismissed by federal courts as a result of this wrongheaded ruling.

Let the case of Terrell McGinnis stand as an example. Ingram Equipment Co., where he worked, had fewer than 15 employees and thus he could not use Title VII. At trial the court found that he "has suffered many more racial indignities at the hands of the Company than any one citizen should be called upon to bear in a lifetime." Even this was understatement. He was removed from his foreman's post because his boss believed that "it just don't (sic) look right ... to have a n-g-er foreman;" he was compelled to clean restrooms and obligated to bar other Black visitors from using the office restrooms; his boss pointed a gun at his head and called him a "black s.o.b." and a "n-g-er"; he was abused physically more than once by his boss (kicking was the preferred mode); and in the midst of lunch break during a business trip in the middle of a restaurant his boss placed his sandwich on the floor and told McGinnis to pick it up, stating "Here you go, my n-g-er."

One should not think that just because the company is located in Birmingham, Alabama, that this is a simple regional phenomenon. In any case the Eleventh Circuit Court of Appeals, following *Patterson*, directed the district court to "reconsider its judgment and award of damages" because "claims of harassment and discriminatory work conditions are no longer actionable under Section 1981."

With their usual flexibility, the Right is seeking to spread this principle beyond the *Patterson* context like a computer virus in order to infect minority business. Recently a court dismissed a complaint alleging that an insurance company had cancelled an agreement to do repair work at a garage because its owners were Black.

The Civil Rights Act of 1991 seeks to reverse discrimination dishonestly foisted upon the nation by the high court. If they had done even a cursory examination of Reconstruction, they would be forced to confront the intellectual dishonesty and distortion of their ruling. For those who are ignorant of the revolutionary impulse that motivated the Civil Rights Act of 1866—and unfortunately that includes the court majority—twisting Section 1981 is no problem. Of course, we know full well that many of the patrons of the court profit handsomely from such distortions. Overturning *Patterson* is a top priority of the Civil Rights Act of 1991.

During the 1990 hearings before the Senate on the bill, Robert Lum, a highly decorated sergeant in the New York City Police Department, spoke eloquently. He was admitted to the force only after a minimum height requirement that unfairly and disparately impacted Asian Americans was overturned in the wake of a 1971 Supreme Court case entitled *Griggs v. Duke Power Co.* He recalled, "When I entered that Police Department, there were only 9 other Asian officers. Presently, there are approximately 180 Asian officers. I assure you not all of them are more than 5 feet 7 inches tall. I remind myself now and then that none of this would have possible if not for a law known as Title Seven...."

It is true that the democratic path calls for equal opportunity as well for racial minorities to enter the police force. Certainly a police force with the same racial composition as a Klan chapter should be avoided, in particular in areas with large numbers of "racial minorities." This became more possible in the wake of *Griggs* in 1971.

To suggest how far this particular high court has retreated, *Griggs* was written by the conservative chief Justice Warren Burger. Indeed, it was held unanimously that Title VII of the Civil Rights Act of 1964 not only bars practices adopted with a discriminatory motive, but also those which allegedly are adopted without discriminatory intent, but have a discriminatory impact on "racial minorities." Thus, Title VII did not allow Duke Power to require a high school diploma or a passing grade on a general intelligence test as a condition of employment or transfer to certain jobs, where both requirements served to invalidate applications of African Americans at a substantially higher rate than white applications and neither requirement was shown to be a "business necessity." To show how far the present court has retreated, it is hard to concede that they could write as Burger did, that such tests were too often an inaccurate measure of the actual ability of African Americans and this was due in part because they had "long received inferior education in segregated schools." Today the right would tend to see that as some sort of "liberal" or "mushy" thinking.

The Kennedy report observes that *Griggs* "has had an extraordinarily positive impact on the American workplace ... For example, the number of black firefighters in the United State more than doubled in the decade after *Griggs*. In addition, the job of police officer has been opened up to tens of thousands of women and racial minorities." Because of *Griggs*, more women have been hired as prison guards; requirements that suggested that a flight attendant must resemble Madonna were dropped; the *Griggs* principle was useful in invalidating provisions that disproportionately afflicted Latinos and Asian Americans, e.g., "accent" requirements and provisos mandating that workers' voices sound a certain way. Despite all this, in 1989 the high court in *Wards Cove Packing Co. v. Atonio* sought to eviscerate *Griggs* and leave the overwhelming majority of this nation to the none too gentle mercies of Bush and his patrons.

What *Wards Cove* sought to do was shift from the boss to the worker the burden of establishing whether a practice with disparate impact is justified. This ignores the salient point that the boss not only often establishes these practices but has uniquely within his possession the files and records that caused these practices to come into being. Too often the boss formulates, evaluates and alters job requirements unilaterally and is consequently in the best position to know what practices may be required by "business necessity." This is so obvious that in 1987 even the Reagan Justice Department acknowledged that the boss should bear the burden of proof as to "business necessity." But this was not good enough for the court.

That is not all. The 1989 high court majority stated that the business purpose served by an employment practice—even a practice that bars virtually all minorities and non-minority women from employment or promotion—need not be "necessary," essential or important. It need only be legitimate and not "mere(ly) insubstantial." Arguably, a boss could suggest that having an accent like William F. Buckley is not "necessary" to be a grocery clerk in Beverly Hills or the Upper East Side of

Manhattan but it is not "merely insubstantial" either and therefore should withstand legal attack.

That is not all. As Senator Kennedy put it, "The Court's opinion places on the complaining party in a disparate impact case the absolute obligation to demonstrate which component or components of a multi-factor employment decision process had a disparate impact, and how great that impact was, even where the employer's failure to maintain adequate data may make it impossible for the complaining party to meet that burden." Moreover, the court avers that the boss has no obligation to maintain such records. So, that the boss can foil claims by burning files is the not so subtle message. In addition, in those cases where a test might be one of many factors in deciding on a promotion or employment, the court makes it easier to rely on an apparently discriminatory test even if one gives lip service to other factors.

The Civil Rights Act of 1991 is designed to reverse (the) discrimination of *Wards Cove* and return the law to 1971.

The National Organization for Women has been in the forefront of the campaign for the Act and was quite active in the movements to stop Robert Bork and David Souter. They are well aware of the Republican Party campaign against the prochoice movement and the right to safe and free abortion. One of the five cases that sparked the promulgation of the Civil Rights Act of 1991 involved Ann Hopkins, who sued her boss (the monopoly accounting firm of choice, Price-Waterhouse) after she was denied promotion because of her gender. This happened though she brought in more business than any of the 87 men being considered for partnership at the time. She was told by one Neanderthal partner that all of her problems at work would be solved if she would "walk more femininely, talk more femininely, dress more femininely, wear make-up, have her hair styled, and wear jewelry."

The court had to decide what effect to give the evidence that Price-Waterhouse allegedly had non-discriminatory reasons for shafting Hopkins. Even the Reagan Justice Department had argued that Title VII was violated whenever there was a discriminatory motive and that the alleged non-discriminatory reasons only limited the remedy, e.g., amount of money damages. But in *Price Waterhouse v. Hopkins*, the high court disagreed and again staked out a position to the right of the Administration. Combined with other court decisions, this allows the boss to possess a racist or sexist motive for not promoting a worker, cloak the decision in alleged non-discriminatory garb—and get away with it.

This shows the contradictory nature of the movement toward "diversity," that has become the latest buzz-word in corporate circles. It is true that more than 3/4 of new entrants to the labor force by the year 2000 will be national minorities and non-minority women and that the force of the labor market is compelling the ruling class to make room for more minority and non-minority women engineers, professors, physicians, etc. This is why billionaires like John Kluge, Walter Annenberg, et. al. give tens of millions of dollars for college scholarships for Blacks. But this is part of the contradictory trajectory. For *Hopkins* shows that racism and sexism still remain useful for keeping these new entrants into the inner sanctum in line, not to mention being a source for increased profit there and elsewhere; and not to mention the prison, homicide,, AIDS, drugs, homelessness, unemployment, etc. that is intended for the bulk of the minority community and a significant percentage of non-minority women. Moreover, *Hopkins* shows that the Right is seeking to supplement their long-term effort to smuggle an intent standard into civil rights law (i.e., it doesn't matter if there was discriminatory impact for a plaintiff to prevail, she must also show the boss intended it) by saying that even if intent does exist, it can be vitiated by other factors. One reads about how the fascist and rightist impulse breeds irrationality and now one can begin to understand this aphorism.

A mass movement helped to propel into office Richard Arrington, the first African-American mayor of Birmingham. He recalled recently, "Birmingham's history of de jure segregation and discrimination against Blacks is well known. Because of such discrimination, Birmingham did not hire its first black police officer until 1966; its first black firefighter was hired in 1968; its second black firefighter was hired in 1974. By the time we entered into the 1981 consent decree, only 13 percent of our police officers and only 9 percent of our firefighters were black in a city that was predominantly black." So, in 1974 and 1975 suits were filed by two groups of private parties and (in those different days) the government of the U.S. , alleging discrimination in the hiring and promotion of Blacks. In 1981 consent decrees were entered (after two trials and judicial findings of racial discrimination) providing goals for the hiring and promotion of Blacks within the Fire Department and other city departments. Notice of all this was given properly and the case was publicized widely.

Then the Birmingham Firefighters Association (BFA) appeared at the hearing filing objections on behalf of Euro-American members; after the hearing but before final approval of the decrees, the BFA and members sought to intervene but this was deemed untimely. Eight months later, more white members sought to overturn the decrees and this action formed the basis for *Martin v. Wilks,* seen by some as the one of the worst of the five 1989 cases.

Prior to the high court opinion it was well-settled that those who failed to intervene in a timely manner when a lawsuit may affect their interests were barred from filing a separate lawsuit challenging the decree. But the Rehnquist court disagreed. Of course, civil rights forces may seek to intervene late at some point too, and it could be argued that Wilks can benefit us; but that is static and "legalistic" thinking for if history tells us anything, it is that courts will distort principle in a second if principle is not in accord with the immediate interests of their patrons.

What *Wilks* does is prevent finality in these complex cases; Birmingham paid $1 million in legal fees alone defending the 1981 decree; today they would have to join as parties in such litigation not only every person currently employed by the affected departments but also *every person* who might seek to be hired or promoted by the department while the decree was pending. Given the state of legal thinking on the right, one wonders if that includes male Euro-American fetuses as well. Don't laugh.

The Civil Rights Act of 1991 seeks to reverse (the) discrimination of *Martin v. Wilks* and return the law to where it was before. It would make the settling of such complex, arduous, expensive lawsuits more orderly and prompt.

Lorrance v. AT&T Technologies represents the catch-22 of the five 1989 court opinions. In 1979 this corporate behemoth adopted a seniority rule that was not applied until 1982 when layoffs took place. Plaintiffs charged at that point that this rule discriminated against women. But the high court ruled that their lawsuit was untimely and they should have filed in 1979. In other words, the Euro-American males in Birmingham can file any time they so choose, while the women of *Lorrance* are not as free to do so. Worse, what this case means is that they could have filed suit in 1979 and been told by the court that they had yet to suffer injury, which in the U.S. makes for a "case," and the suit was not ripe; or they file in 1982 and are told that they are too late and should have filed in 1979. As Senator Kennedy put it, "... the *Lorrance* rule (logically) would bar challenges to contemporary applications of discriminatory rules adopted prior to 1965—that is, all the discriminatory rules in existence when Title VII became effective—because the deadline for timely charge would have expired before Title VII ever came into effect." This would work to freeze discrimination into place like a tableau in a museum and, correspondingly, only guarantee that an already tottering economy would continue to teeter.

Current law also provides a generally longer statute of limitations for claims of intentional race discrimination than for other forms of discrimination in employment. It is the opinion of civil rights forces that this is an anomaly that should be corrected, along with other presumed warps imbedded in statutes of limitations. The Act would seek to undermine the saying that a woman has to be twice as good to get half as far.

The case of Patricia Swanson suggests why civil rights forces are moving against other anomalies within the law. Her testimony before Senator Kennedy's committee was riveting: "(My) boss ... would sneak up behind me and try to unhook my bra. This happened at least 2 to 3 times a week. Sometimes I had to scoot down in my chair to keep him from succeeding. Even then he would reach down the chair and keep trying.... On several occasions, (he) would run up behind me in the hallway and would put his hand under my skirt and grab me between the legs, on my thigh. One time I was carrying a cup of hot coffee when he did this, and spilled it down the front of me. He told me to take my clothes off right there and he would have them cleaned. I went into the ladies room to clean up in private, and he followed me. As I was wiping the coffee off my blouse, he tried to take the paper towel out of my hand and wipe off my chest himself. He didn't leave until I started to cry ... on several occasions, (he) called me in to his office ... when other men were present. They were salesmen, customer friends of his, or whole-salers. When I entered he would point at me and say to the other men present, 'Have you ever seen such big boobs; wouldn't you love to grab them?' I never knew who these men were. My husband was in the automobile business too, and they might have known him. I was humiliated, and worried that my husband might be as well.... All this harassment had a strong effect on me ... he would make me cry—I would always go into the washroom to do it, so that he wouldn't see me. I was always afraid of running into (him).... I felt like I was a prisoner in my own office.... Sometimes the harassment would give me migraines. After one particularly bad incident, my migraine was so bad that I almost passed out."

The district court found that there was sexual harassment, but ruled that she was dismissed from her job for unrelated reasons. But it did give her attorney's fees and nominal damages of $1.

On appeal the Seventh Circuit Court of Appeals affirmed the finding of sexual harassment but reversed the judgment for attorney's fees and nominal damages. In an anomalous fashion the court ruled that the boss had violated Title VII but that Swanson could not get relief; so she wound up paying her boss's court costs too!

Swanson's case is not an isolated one. Ask Hortencia Bohen of East Chicago, Indiana. She was the victim of atrocious sexual harassment at the hands of her supervisor and coworkers. She was hit with verbal abuse, unwanted touching, and was told that she should be raped! The court ruled that "sexual harassment was the general, ongoing and accepted practice" at the fire department where she worked as a dispatcher; but she could not recover damages under Title VII.

The Civil Rights Act of 1991 seeks to reverse discrimination by making suit for damages as a remedy for all forms of intentional discrimination. It seeks to relieve the agony of Patricia Swanson and Hortencia Bohen and millions of saying that a woman has to be twice as good to get half as far.

Plaintiffs often have to rely on the private bar to obtain justice but as the case of Swanson demonstrates, recovering attorney's fees can be difficult, which has the added impact of making it more difficult to fight discrimination through legal means. One can easily speculate that this has the ripple effect of increasing crime and other forms of "anti-social" behavior that the right so frequently rails against. In addition to removing some of the obstacles to receiving attorney's fees (which would also aid a sector of small business that has been a key ally of the working class in the U.S.), the Civil Rights Act of 1991 would also make for appropriate adjustments for delay of payment of attorney's fees. We know that big business tries to starve the solo attorneys who bring many of these cases by delaying payment well beyond entering of judgment.

A titanic struggle forced the passage of this important legislation but barely after signing it, the White House was seeking to undermine it. The *Washington Post* of 21 November 1991 reported the dispiriting news that on the day Bush was scheduled to sign the bill, his staff circulated to federal agencies and departments a sweeping directive that would eliminate all affirmative action policies. The directive also would have terminated the "Uniform Guidelines on Employee Selection Procedures," used by the private and public sectors to determine how to comply with laws banning job discrimination. This bizarre proviso would have banned affirmative action. The directive was characterized as a "signing statement" to be attached to the Civil Rights Act, underscoring the administration's destructive interpretation. A firestorm of protest erupted that forced the Administration to beat a rapid retreat. Still, it was clear that the Administration's effort to gut affirmative action continues unabated. The *New Republic* of 16 December 1991 reported that devilish and arcane interpretations are still being put forward by the White House in order to destroy affirmative action.

As ever, the White House is serving as a puppet for big business. They fought vigorously to make sure that caps on compensatory and punitive damages remained on the amount that women and the disabled could recover in employment discrimination suits. Advocates of women's equity, on the other hand, are looking forward to exercising their newly found rights under the act. On the other hand, progressive forces are concerned that language in the act seeking to outlaw "race norming" in testing might vitiate steps toward affirmative action, particularly in police and fire departments.

The fight for the Civil Rights Act of 1991 could well be deemed a crucial turning point for the progressive forces of the U.S. Moreover, we should simultaneously ponder seriously the role of the Supreme Court and whether reform and renewal are needed for this body; we should also strive to remind those who see the U.S. as the citadel of "human rights" to study the Bush veto and the concomitant havoc it has caused in the lives of millions. Civil rights, labor and women's forces and their allies must prepare to trump the attempt by Bush and his clique to play the race card.

Affirmative action is an absolute necessity if the struggle for democracy is to survive. Excluding categorically racially oppressed and ethnic minorities and non-minority women is a blow to the future of this nation, not to mention a crime against those who have to endure bias. Affirmative action in expanding democracy represents a step toward socialism. It is a battle that must be taken up with more vigor by trade unions and all who are fair-minded.

Notes

INTRODUCTION

1. Professor Arthur Kinoy of Rutgers Law School, the National Lawyers Guild, the Center for Constitutional Rights and the National Conference of Black Lawyers formed the Affirmative Action Coordinating Center and argued vigorously in a number of brief s that the 13th Amendment should be relied on to justify affirmative action in that its reach and impact would be more significant than the 14th Amendment. Cf., e.g., *United Steelworkers of America v. Weber*, 443 US 193 (1979), *Regents of University of California v. Bakke*, 438 US 265 (1978).
2. Karl Marx, *Capital, Vol. I*, chapter 10, section 7.
3. *United Steelworkers of America v. Weber*, 443 US 193 (1979).

CHAPTER 1

1. *Santa Barbara News Press*, 19 December 1991.
2. *New York Times*, 5 June 1991; *New York Newsday*, 5 June 1991.
3. *New York Times*, 29 July 1991.
4. *Los Angeles Times*, 23 May 1991.
5. *Los Angeles Times*, 29 July 1991.
6. *New York Times*, 11 November 1991.
7. *Santa Barbara News Press*, 30 November 1991.
8. *Washington Post*, 28 November 1991.
9. *Los Angeles Times*, 9 August 1991.
10. *New York Times*, 20 August 1991.
11. *Los Angeles Times*, 14 September 1991; *City Sun* (NY), 7-13 August 1991: "Blacks, who constitute 13.2% of the U.S. population in the 20-29 age band, accounted for only 5.7% of the 1990 medical school graduating class. Mexican-Americans in 1990 were 7.1% of the age band and 1.6% of the graduates. The comparable ratios in 1990 figures for mainland Puerto Ricans were 1.3 percent and 0.6 percent; and for Native Americans, 0.9 percent and 0.3 percent."
12. *New York Times*, 22 November 1991.
13. *Los Angeles Times*, 7 January 1992.
14. *Los Angeles Times*, 23 May 1991.
15. *North Star: The Voice of Today's African-American*, October 1991.
16. *Jet*, 9 March 1992.
17. *Black Enterprise*, October 1991.
18. *New York Times*, 30 September 1991.
19. *Insight*, 11 November 1991.
20. *National Law Journal*, 25 November 1991.
21. *Chronicle of Higher Education*, 4 December 1991.
22. *New York Times*, 15 August 1991.
23. *Guardian*, 5 February 1992; *New York Times*, 18 December 1991; *Washington Post*, 11 October 1991.
24. *Business Week*, 16 December 1991.
25. *New York Times*, 30 May 1991; *New York Times*, 14 December 1991.
26. *New York Times*, 26 September 1991.

27. *Washington Post*, 30 August 1991; *Los Angeles Times*, 30 August 1991.
28. *Los Angeles Times*, 21 October 1991.
29. *New York Times*, 3 October 1991.
30. *Los Angeles Times*, 9 September 1991.
31. Hillel Levine and Lawrence Harmon, *The Death of an American Jewish Community: A Tragedy of Good Intentions*, New York: Free Press, 1992.
32. *Jet*, 9 September 1991.
33. *Chronicle of Higher Education*, 9 October 1991.
34. *New York Times*, 13 September 1991
35. *Washington Post*, 29 February 1991.
36. *Chronicle of Higher Education*, 4 December 1991; *Washington Post*, 5 March 1992.
37. *UC Focus*, January 1992.
38. *Los Angeles Times*, 21 August 1991.
39. *Las Angeles Times*, 4 November 1991.

CHAPTER 2
1. *Chronicle of Higher Education*, 8 January 1992.
2. *North Star*, June 1991.
3. *Los Angeles Sentinel*, 5 December 1991.
4. *Santa Barbara News Press*, 25 August 1991.
5. *New York Amsterdam News*, 30 November 1991.
6. *New York Times*, 26 September 1991.
7. *Black Enterprise*, August 1991.
8. *Los Angeles Times*, 9 August 1991; William P. O'Hare, et. al., "African Americans in the 1990s," *Population Bulletin* vol. 46, no. 1, (Washington, DC: Population Reference Bureau, Inc., 1991). cf. also, Douglas Massey and Mitchell L. Eggers, "The Ecology of Inequality: Minorities and the Concentration of Poverty, 19701980," *American Journal of Sociology*, 95 (March 1990): 1153—1188. Reynolds Farley and Walter R. Allen, *The Color Line and the Quality of Life in America*, (New York: Russell Sage Foundation, 1987).
9. *Washington Post*, 27 August 1991.
10. *New York Times*, 23 September 1991.
11. *New York Times*, 10 December 1991.
12. *New York Amsterdam News*, 17 August 1991.
13. *Jet*, 9 December 1991.
14. *Washington Post*, 24 August 1991.
15. *New York Times*, 5 March 1992.
16. *Washington Post*, 5 March 1992.
17. *Washington Post*, 16 October 1991.
18. *Washington Post*, 28 February 1992.
19. *Los Angeles Times*, 24 November 1991.
20. *New York Times*, 17 December 1991; *New York Times*, 29 November 1991; *New York Times*, 2 December 1991.
21. *Washington Post*, 2 November 1991.
22. *New York Times*, 5 December 1991; *Washington Post*, 5 December 1991.
23. *Washington Post*, 5 February 1992; *Washington Post*, 10 March 1992.

24. *Los Angeles Times,* 2 November 1990.
25. *Washington Post,* 23 August 1991; *National Law Journal,* 26 August 1991.
26. *New York Newsday,* 22 October 1990; *New York Times,* 14 December 1991.
27. *Los Angeles Times,* 3 November 1991.

CHAPTER 3

1. *Washington Post,* 20 September 1991.
2. *San Francisco Bay Guardian,* 27 June 1990.
3. *Off Our Backs,* July 1990.
4. *Business Week,* 27 November 1989.
5. *Business Week,* 27 January 1992; New York Times, 12 February 1992.
6. *Los Angeles Times,* 14 November 1991.
7. *Los Angeles Times,* 28 August 1991.
8. *Los Angeles Times,* 5 February 1991; Cf. also, Rita Mae Kelly and Jane Bayes, eds., *Comparable Worth, Pay Equity and Public Policy,* Westport: Greenwood, 1991.
9. *Jet,* 19 May 1990.
10. *New York Amsterdam News,* 19 May 1990.
11. *Jet,* 9 September 1991.
12. *Weekly Mail,* 5-11 July 1991.
13. *Business Week,* 16 July 1990.
14. *New York Times,* 10 December 1991.
15. *Los Angeles Times,* 16 January 1992.
16. *New Directions for Women,* November-December 1991.
17. *People,* 9 December 1991; *Los Angeles Times,* 29 September 1991.
18. *Los Angeles Times,* 10 February 1992.
19. *Washington Post,* 26 August 1991; *New York Newsday,* 26 August 1991.
20. *Business Week,* 2 September 1991.
21. *Los Angeles Times,* 25 August 1991.
22. *Washington Post,* 12 January 1992.
23. *New York Times,* 10 September 1991.
24. *Washington Post,* 18 February 1992.
25. *National Law Journal,* 11 December 1989.
26. *Chronicle of Higher Education,* 9 October 1991.
27. *New York Times,* 20 February 1992; *New York Times,* 3 October 1991.
28. *Guardian,* 4 March 1992.
29. *New York Times,* 8 November 1991.
30. *New York Times,* 18 February 1992.
31. *Los Angeles Times,* 6 January 1992.
32. *Los Angeles Times,* 21 January 1992.
33. *Washington Post,* 3 September 1991.
34. *Los Angeles Times,* 19 February 1992.
35. *Los Angeles Times,* 9 January 1992.
36. *Chronicle of Higher Education,* 26 February 1992; *Los Angeles Times,* 28 August 1991.
37. *Los Angeles Times,* 12 March 1992.
38. *Washington Post,* 29 February 1992.
39. *New York Times,* 18 January 1992.

40. *San Francisco Chronicle,* 18 March 1990.
41. *Chronicle of Higher Education,* 2 October 1991.

CHAPTER 4

1. *Los Angeles Times,* 19 September 1991.
2. *Los Angeles Times,* 20 September 1991.
3. *Los Angeles Sentinel,* 29 August 1991.
4. *San Francisco Bay Guardian,* 19 June 1991.
5. *Los Angeles Times,* 1 September 1991.
6. *Black Enterprise,* November 1991.
7. *Black Enterprise,* February 1992.
8. *Black Enterprise,* March 1992.
9. *Black Enterprise,* December 1991.
10. *Los Angeles Times,* 20 August 1991.
11. *New York Times,* 16 February 1992.
12. *New York Times,* 11 December 1991.
13. *Washington Post,* 22 October 1991; *Black Enterprise,* February 1992.
14. *Los Angeles Times,* 12 October 1991.
15. *Los Angeles Sentinel,* 4 March 1992; *Emerge,* March 1992.
16. New York Times, 23 December 1991.

Index